Meeting the Needs

of Your Most Able Pupils:

SCIENCE

Other titles in the series

Meeting the Needs
of Your Most Able Pupils:
SCIENCE

Tim Alderman

Routledge
Taylor & Francis Group

LONDON AND NEW YORK

First published 2008 by
Routledge
2 Park Square, Milton Park, Abingdon, Oxon OX14 4RN

Simultaneously published in the USA and Canada by
Routledge
270 Madison Ave, New York, NY 10016

Routledge is an imprint of Taylor & Francis, an informa business

British Library Cataloguing in Publication data
A catalogue record for this book is available from the British Library

Library of Congress Cataloging in Publication Data
A catalog record has been requested

ISBN 13: 978 1 84312 277 7 (pbk)
ISBN 13: 978 0 203 93230 7 (ebk)
ISBN 10: 1 84312 277 4 (pbk)
ISBN 10: 0 203 93230 7 (ebk)

Series production editors: Sarah Fish and Andrew Welsh
Typeset by Servis Filmsetting Ltd, Manchester
Printed and bound in Great Britain
by Bell & Bain Ltd, Glasgow

*This book is dedicated to Margaret, Matthew, Anthony and Edward.
I could write this book because they thought I could.*

Contents

Acknowledgements

This book was written with help and guidance from Gwen Goodhew, who showed extreme patience and support. It is a culmination of some extensive research but, more importantly, many years of collaboration with fellow G&T professionals across schools in Merseyside who have provided a diverse range of opportunities for able students. I have gained tremendously from their input, as have thousands of students. My thanks go to them.

Contributors to the series

The author

Tim Alderman is deputy headteacher at a large community school in Liverpool. Prior to this he worked, since the inception of Excellence in Cities (EiC) in 1999, as the cluster coordinator for gifted and talented in both the north and south of Liverpool whilst working as a science teacher in two different schools. He has also worked as a head of science and played an active role in the EiC initiative in the North West, providing INSET for other coordinators and local teachers.

Series editor

Gwen Goodhew's many and varied roles within the field of gifted and talented education have included school G&T coordinator, director of Wirral Able Children Centre, Knowsley Excellence in Cities (EiC) G&T coordinator, member of the DfES G&T Advisory Group, teacher trainer and consultant. She has written and edited numerous reports and articles on the subject and co-authored *Providing for Able Children* with Linda Evans.

Other authors

Art

Kim Earle is a former secondary head of art and design and is currently an able pupils and arts consultant for St Helens. She has been a member of DfES steering groups, is an Artsmark validator, a subject editor for G&TWISE and a practising designer jeweller and enameller.

Design and Technology

During the writing of the book **Louise T. Davies** was a part-time subject adviser for design and technology at the QCA (Qualifications and Curriculum Authority), and part of the KS3 National Strategy team for the D&T programme. She has authored over 40 D&T books and award-winning multimedia resources. She is currently deputy chief executive of the Design and Technology Association.

English

Erica Glew teaches English throughout the secondary age range to GCSE, AS and A level. She is the gifted and talented coordinator and head of the learning resources centre at the Holy Trinity C of E secondary school, a specialist comprehensive school in West Sussex. Erica is also an examiner team leader in English Literature at A level.

Geography

Jane Ferretti is a lecturer in education at the University of Sheffield working in initial teacher training. Until 2003 she was head of geography at King Edward VII School, Sheffield, a large 11–18 comprehensive, and was also involved in gifted and talented initiatives at the school and with the local authority. Jane has co-authored a number of A level geography textbooks and a GCSE revision book and is one of the editors of *Wideworld* magazine. She is a member of the Geographical Association and a contributor to their journals *Teaching Geography* and *Geography*.

History

Steven Barnes is a former head of history at a secondary school and Secondary Strategy consultant for the School Improvement Service in Lincolnshire. He has written history exemplifications for Assessment for Learning for the Secondary National Strategy. He is now an assistant head with responsibility for teaching and learning for a school in Lincolnshire.

Mathematics

Lynne McClure is an independent consultant in the field of mathematics education and G&T. She works with teachers and students in schools all over the UK and abroad as well as Warwick, Cambridge, Oxford Brookes and Edinburgh Universities. Lynne edits several maths and education journals.

Jennifer Piggott is a lecturer in mathematics enrichment and communication technology at Cambridge University. She is Director of the NRICH mathematics project and is part of the eastern region coordination team for the NCETM (National Centre for Excellence in the Teaching of Mathematics). Jennifer is an experienced mathematics and ICT teacher.

Modern Foreign Languages

Gretchen Ingram is a former head of department with wide experience of teaching, learning and examining modern foreign languages in various UK comprehensive schools.

Music

Jonathan Savage is a senior lecturer in music education at the Institute of Education, Manchester Metropolitan University. Until 2001 he was head of music at Debenham High School, an 11–16 comprehensive school in Suffolk. He is a co-author of a new resource introducing computer game sound design to the Key Stage 3 curriculum (www.sound2game.net) and managing director of UCan.tv (www.ucan.tv), a company specialising in the production of educational software and hardware. When not doing all of this, he is busy parenting four very musically talented children!

Physical Education and Sport

David Morley has taught physical education in a number of secondary schools. He is currently senior lecturer in physical education at Leeds Metropolitan University and the director of the national DfES-funded 'Development in PE' project which is part of the Gifted and Talented strand of the PE, School Sport and Club Links (PESSCL) project. He is also a member of the team responsible for developing resources for national Multi-skill Clubs and is the founder and director of the Carnegie Regional Multi-skill Camp held at Leeds Met Carnegie.

Richard Bailey is professor of pedagogy at Roehampton University, having previously worked at Reading and Leeds Metropolitan University, and at Canterbury Christ Church University where he was director of the Centre for Physical Education Research. He is a well-known author and speaker on physical education, sport and education.

Religious Education

Dilwyn Hunt has worked as a specialist RE adviser in Birmingham and Dudley in the West Midlands, and has a wide range of teaching experience. He is currently a school adviser with responsibility for gifted and talented pupils.

Online content on the Routledge website

The online material accompanying this book may be used by the purchasing individual/organisation only. The files may be amended to suit particular situations, or individual learning needs, and printed out for use by the purchaser. The material can be accessed at www.routledge.com/education/fultonresources.asp.

01 Institutional quality standards in gifted and talented education
02 Policy for able students in science
03 Auditing provision for the most able students in science at KS3/4
04 Departmental action plan for improving provision for the most able
05 Example of a scheme of work incorporating African Caribbean culture
06 Progress log for gifted and talented students in science
07 Science individual learning plan
08 Coursework writing frame
09 PowerPoint presentation for departmental INSET
10 Preferred learning styles – a quick questionnaire
11 Teaching styles and techniques
12 High ability checklist
13 Lesson plan pro-forma
14 Lesson plan – properties of materials
15 Activity sheet – comparing natural and synthetic material
16 Risk assessment for educational visits
17 SETPOINT: list of organisations

www.routledge.com/education

Introduction

Who should use this book?

This book is for all teachers of science working with Key Stage 3 and Key Stage 4 pupils. It will be relevant to teachers working within the full spectrum of schools, from highly selective establishments to comprehensive and secondary modern schools as well as some special schools. Its overall objective is to provide a practical resource that heads of department, gifted and talented coordinators, leading teachers for gifted and talented education and classroom teachers can use to develop a coherent approach to provision for their most able pupils.

Why is it needed?

School populations differ greatly and pupils considered very able in one setting might not stand out in another. Nevertheless, whatever the general level of ability within a school, there has been a tendency to plan and provide for the middle range, to modify for those who are struggling and to leave the most able to 'get on with it'. This has meant that the most able have:

- not been sufficiently challenged and stimulated
- underachieved
- been unaware of what they might be capable of achieving
- been unaware of what they need to do to achieve at the highest level
- not had high enough ambitions and aspirations
- sometimes become disaffected.

How will this book help teachers?

This book and its accompanying website will, through its combination of practical ideas, materials for photocopying or downloading, and case studies:

- help teachers of science to focus on the top 5–10% of the ability range in their particular school and to find ways of providing for these pupils, both within and beyond the classroom
- equip them with strategies and ideas to support exceptionally able pupils, i.e. those in the top 5% nationally.

Terminology

Since there is confusion about the meaning of the words 'gifted' and 'talented', the terms 'more able', 'most able' and 'exceptionally able' will generally be used in this series.

When 'gifted' and 'talented' are used, the definitions provided by the Department for Education and Skills (DfES) in its Excellence in Cities programme will apply. That is:

- **gifted** pupils are the most academically able in a school. This ability might be general or specific to a particular subject area, such as mathematics.

- **talented** pupils are those with high ability or potential in art, music, performing arts or sport.

The two groups together should form 5–10% of any school population.

There are, of course, some pupils who are both gifted and talented. Examples that come to mind are the budding physicist who plays the violin to a high standard in his spare time, or the pupil with high general academic ability who plays for the area football team.

This book is part of a series dealing with providing challenge for the most able secondary age pupils in a range of subjects. It is likely that some of the books in the series might also contain ideas that would be relevant to teachers of science.

CHAPTER 1

Our more able pupils – the national scene

- Making good provision for the most able – what's in it for schools?
- National initiatives since 1997
- *Every Child Matters* and the Children Act 2004
- *Higher Standards, Better Schools for All* – Education White Paper, October 2005
- Self-evaluation and inspection
- Resources for teachers and parents of more able pupils

Today's gifted pupils are tomorrow's social, intellectual, economic and cultural leaders and their development cannot be left to chance.

(Deborah Eyre, director of the National Academy for Gifted and Talented Youth, 2004)

The debate about whether to make special provision for the most able pupils in secondary schools ran its course during the last decade of the twentieth century. Explicit provision to meet their learning needs is now considered neither elitist nor a luxury. From an inclusion angle these pupils must have the same chances as others to develop their potential to the full. We know from international research that focusing on the needs of the most able changes teachers' perceptions of the needs of all their pupils, and there follows a consequential rise in standards. But for teachers who are not convinced by the inclusion or school improvement arguments, there is a much more pragmatic reason for meeting the needs of able pupils. Of course, it is preferable that colleagues share a common willingness to address the needs of the most able, but if they don't, it can at least be pointed out that, quite simply, it is something that all teachers are now required to do, not an optional extra.

All schools should seek to create an atmosphere in which to excel is not only acceptable but desirable.

(*Excellence in Schools* – DfEE 1997)

> High achievement is determined by 'the school's commitment to inclusion and the steps it takes to ensure that every pupil does as well as possible'.
>
> (*Handbook for Inspecting Secondary Schools* – Ofsted 2003)

A few years ago, efforts to raise standards in schools concentrated on getting as many pupils as possible over the Level 5 hurdle at the end of Key Stage 3 and over the 5 A*–C grades hurdle at GCSE. Resources were pumped into borderline pupils and the most able were not, on the whole, considered a cause for concern. The situation has changed dramatically in the last nine years with schools being expected to set targets for A*s and As and to show added value by helping pupils entering the school with high SATs scores to achieve Levels 7 and beyond, if supporting data suggests that that is what is achievable. Early recognition of high potential and the setting of curricular targets are at last addressing the lack of progress demonstrated by many able pupils in Year 7 and more attention is being paid to creating a climate in which learning can flourish. But there is a push for even more support for the most able through the promotion of personalised learning.

> The goal is that five years from now: gifted and talented students progress in line with their ability rather than their age; schools inform parents about tailored provision in an annual school profile; curricula include a gifted and talented dimension and at 14–19 there is more stretch and differentiation at the top end, so no matter what your talent it will be engaged; and the effect of poverty on achievement is reduced, because support for high-ability students from poorer backgrounds enables them to thrive.
>
> (Speech at National Academy for Gifted and Talented Youth – David Miliband, Minister for State for School Standards, May 2004)

It is hoped that this book, with the others in this series, will help to accelerate these changes.

Making good provision for the most able – what's in it for schools?

Schools and/or subject departments often approach provision for the most able pupils with some reluctance because they imagine a lot of extra work for very little reward. In fact, the rewards of providing for these pupils are substantial.

- It can be very stimulating to the subject specialist to explore ways of developing approaches with enthusiastic and able students.

> Taking a serious look at what I should expect from the most able and then at how I should teach them has given my teaching a new lease of life. I feel so sorry for youngsters who were taught by me ten years ago. They must have been bored beyond belief. But then, to be quite honest, so was I.
>
> (Science teacher)

- Offering opportunities to tackle work in a more challenging manner often interests pupils whose abilities have gone unnoticed because they have not been motivated by a bland educational diet.

  > Some of the others were invited to an after-school maths club. When I heard what they were doing, it sounded so interesting that I asked the maths teacher if I could go too. She was a bit doubtful at first because I have messed about a lot but she agreed to take me on trial. I'm one of her star pupils now and she reckons I'll easily get an A*. I still find some of the lessons really slow and boring but I don't mess around – well, not too much.
  >
  > (Year 10 boy)

- When pupils are engaged by the work they are doing motivation, attainment and discipline improve.

  > You don't need to be gifted to work out that the work we do is much more interesting and exciting. It's made others want to be like us.
  >
  > (Comment of a student involved in an extension programme for the most able)

- Schools identified as very good by Ofsted generally have good provision for their most able students.

  > If you are willing to deal effectively with the needs of able pupils you will raise the achievement of all pupils.
  >
  > (Mike Tomlinson, former director of Ofsted)

- The same is true of individual departments in secondary schools. All those considered to be very good have spent time developing a sound working approach that meets the needs of their most able pupils.

  > The department creates a positive atmosphere by its organisation, display and the way that students are valued. Learning is generally very good and often excellent throughout the school. The teachers' high expectations permeate the atmosphere and are a significant factor in raising achievement. These expectations are reflected in the curriculum which has depth and students are able and expected to experience difficult problems in all year groups.
  >
  > (Mathematics Department, Hamstead Hall School, Birmingham; Ofsted 2003)

National initiatives since 1997

In 1997, the new government demonstrated its commitment to gifted and talented education by setting up a Gifted and Talented Advisory Group (GTAG). Since then there has been a wide range of government and government-funded initiatives that have, either directly or indirectly, impacted on our most able pupils and their teachers. Details of some can be found below. Others that relate to science will be found later in this book.

Excellence in Cities

In an attempt to deal with the chronic underachievement of able pupils in inner city areas, Excellence in Cities (EiC) was launched in 1999. This was a very ambitious, well-funded programme with many different strands. In the first place it concentrated on secondary age pupils but work was extended into the primary sector in many areas. Provision for gifted and talented students was one of the strands.

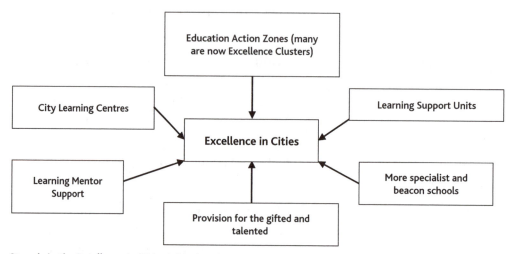

Strands in the Excellence in Cities Initiative

EiC schools were expected to:

- develop a whole-school policy for their most able pupils

- appoint a gifted and talented coordinator with sufficient time to fulfil the role

- send the coordinator on a national training programme run by Oxford Brookes University

- identify 5–10% of pupils in each year group as their gifted and talented cohort, the gifted being the academically able and the talented being those with latent or obvious ability in PE, sport, music, art or the performing arts

- provide an appropriate programme of work both within the school day and beyond

- set 'aspirational' targets both for the gifted and talented cohort as a whole and for individual pupils

- work with other schools in a 'cluster' to provide further support for these pupils

- work with other agencies, such as Aimhigher, universities, businesses and private sector schools, to enhance provision and opportunities for these pupils.

Funding changes have meant that schools no longer receive dedicated EiC money through local authorities but the lessons learned from EiC have been influential in developing a national approach to gifted and talented education. **All** schools are now expected to adopt similar strategies to ensure that the needs of their most able students are met.

Excellence Clusters

Although EiC was set up initially in the main urban conurbations, other hot spots of underachievement and poverty were also identified and Excellence Clusters were established. For example, Ellesmere Port, Crewe and Barrow-in-Furness are pockets of deprivation, with major social problems and significant underachievement, in otherwise affluent areas. Excellence Clusters have been established in these three places and measures are being taken to improve provision for the most able pupils. The approach is similar to that used in Excellence in Cities areas.

Aimhigher

Aimhigher is another initiative of the Department for Education and Skills (DfES) working in partnership with the Higher Education Funding Council for England (HEFCE). Its remit is to widen participation in UK higher education, particularly among students from groups that do not have a tradition of going to university, such as some ethnic minorities, the disabled and those from poorer homes. Both higher education institutions and secondary schools have Aimhigher coordinators who work together to identify pupils who would benefit from additional support and to plan a programme of activities. Opportunities are likely to include:

- mentoring, including e-mentoring
- residential summer schools
- visits to different campuses and university departments
- masterclasses
- online information for students and parents
- advice on the wide range of financial and other support available to disadvantaged students.

One national Aimhigher project, Higher Education Gateway, is specifically targeted on gifted and talented students from disadvantaged groups. More information can be found at www.aimhigher.ac.uk.

National Academy for Gifted and Talented Youth (NAGTY)

Government initiatives have not been confined to the most able pupils in deprived areas. In 2002, the National Academy for Gifted and Talented Youth was established at Warwick University. Its brief was to offer support to the most able 5% of the school population and their teachers and parents. It did this in a number of ways:

National Academy for Gifted and Talented Youth		
Student Academy	**Professional Academy**	**Expertise Centre**
• Summer schools including link-ups with CTY in USA. • Outreach courses in a wide range of subjects at universities and other venues across the country. • Online activities – currently maths, classics, ethics, philosophy.	• Continuing professional development for teachers. • A PGCE+ programme for trainee teachers. • Ambassador School Programme to disseminate good practice amongst schools.	• Leading research in gifted and talented education.

NAGTY worked closely with the DfES with the latter setting policy and NAGTY increasingly taking the lead in the practical application of this policy – a policy known as the English Model, which, as explained on NAGTY's website, is 'rooted in day-to-day classroom provision and enhanced by additional, more advanced opportunities offered both within school and outside of it'. NAGTY ceased operation in August 2007 and was replaced by the Young, Gifted and Talented Programme (see below).

The Young, Gifted and Talented Programme (YG&T)

In December 2006, the UK government announced the creation of a new programme in England, the National Programme for Gifted and Talented Education (NPGATE), to be managed by CfBT Education Trust and now known as the Young, Gifted & Talented Programme (YG&T). Among the changes proposed are:

- a much greater emphasis on school and local level provision.

- the setting-up of Excellence Hubs – HEI-led partnerships to provide non-residential summer schools and a diverse range of outreach provision, including summer activities, weekend events and online and blended learning models. There will be free places for the disadvantaged.

- the appointment of gifted and talented leading teachers – one for each secondary school and each cluster of primary schools.

- a national training programme for gifted and talented leading teachers organised by the national primary and secondary strategies.

Further information about YG&T can be found at www.dfes.gov.uk/ygt or www.cfbt.com.

Gifted and talented summer schools

Education authorities are encouraged to work in partnership with schools to run a number of summer schools (dependent on the size of the authority) for the most able pupils in Years 6–11. It is expected that there will be a particular emphasis on transition and that around 50 hours of tuition will be offered. Some schools and authorities run summer schools for up to ten days whilst others cover a shorter period and have follow-up sessions or even residential weekends later in the school year. Obviously the main aim is to challenge and stimulate these pupils but the DfES also hopes that:

- they will encourage teachers and advisers to adopt innovative teaching approaches

- teachers will continue to monitor these pupils over time

- where Year 6 pupils are involved, it will make secondary teachers aware of what they can achieve and raise their expectations of Year 7 pupils.

More can be found out about these summer schools at www.standards.dfes. gov.uk/giftedandtalented. Funding for them has now been incorporated into the school development grant.

Regional partnerships

When Excellence in Cities (EiC) was first introduced, gifted and talented strand coordinators from different EiC partnerships began to meet up with others in their regions to explore ways of working together so that the task was more manageable and resources could be pooled. One of the most successful examples of cooperation was the Trans-Pennine Group that started up in the northwest. It began to organise training on a regional basis as well as masterclasses and other activities for some gifted and talented pupils. The success of this and other groups led to the setting-up of nine regional partnerships with initial support from NAGTY and finance from DfES. Each partnership had a steering group composed of representatives from local authorities, higher education institutions, regional organisations concerned with gifted and talented children and NAGTY. Each regional partnership organised professional training; sought to support schools and areas in greatest need; tried to ensure that all 11- to 19-year-olds who fell into the top 5% of the ability range were registered with NAGTY; provided opportunities for practitioner research and arranged challenging activities for pupils. Under the YG&T Programme, nine Excellence Hubs have been created to continue and expand the work of the regional partnerships.

Every Child Matters: Change for Children and the Children Act 2004

The likelihood of all children reaching their potential has always been hampered by the fragmented nature of agencies concerned with provision for them. Vital information held by an agency about a child's needs has often in the past been kept back from other agencies, including schools. This has had a particularly negative impact on the disadvantaged, for example, looked-after children. In 2004, 57% of looked-after children left school without even one GCSE or GNVQ and only 6% achieved five or more good GCSEs (see national statistics at www.dfes.gov.uk/rsgateway/). This represents a huge waste of national talent as well as many personal tragedies.

The Children Act 2004 sought to overcome these problems by, amongst other things, requiring:

- local authorities to make arrangements to promote cooperation between agencies to ensure the well-being of all children

- all children's services to bear these five outcomes in mind when planning provision. Children should:

  - be healthy

  - stay safe

  - enjoy and achieve

  - make a positive contribution

  - achieve economic well-being.

There are major implications for schools in seeking to achieve these outcomes for their most able pupils, especially where there is deprivation and/or low aspiration:

- local authorities to appoint a director of children's services to coordinate education and social services

- each local authority to take on the role of corporate parent to promote the educational achievement of looked-after children. This should help to ensure that greater consideration is given to their education when changes in foster placements are being considered

- the setting-up of an integrated inspection regime to look at the totality of provision for children.

More information can be found at www.everychildmatters.gov.uk.

Higher Standards, Better Schools for All (Education White Paper, October 2005)

Although the thrust of this Education White Paper is to improve educational opportunities for all, there is no doubt that some proposals will particularly benefit the most able, especially those that are disadvantaged in some way.

- Pupils receiving free school meals will be able to get **free public transport** to any one of three secondary schools closest to their homes between two and six miles away. At present, such children have very little choice in secondary schooling because their parents cannot afford the fares. This measure will allow them access to schools that might be better able to cater for their particular strengths and needs.

- **The National Register of Gifted and Talented Learners** will record the top 5% of the nation's children, as identified by a wide range of measures, so that they can be tracked and supported throughout their school careers. At first, the focus will be on 11- to 19-year-olds but later identification will start at the age of 4. As a first step, in 2006 all secondary schools were asked to identify gifted and talented students in the school census. In reality, some authorities had already begun this monitoring process but making it a national priority will bring other schools and authorities up to speed.

- In line with new school managerial structures, **'leading teachers' of the gifted and talented** will take the place of gifted and talented coordinators. Training (optionally accredited) will be organised through the national strategies. Leading teachers will work closely with School Improvement Partners and local authority coordinators to implement G&T improvement plans, and undertake much of the work previously undertaken by school coordinators.

- **Additional training** in providing for gifted and talented pupils will be available to all schools.

- **A national programme of non-residential summer schools** will be organised to run alongside gifted and talented summer schools already provided by local authorities and individual schools.

- Secondary schools will be encouraged to make greater use of **grouping by ability** in order to meet the needs of the most able and to use **curriculum flexibility** to allow pupils to take Key Stage 3 tests and GCSE courses early and to mix academic and vocational courses.

- **At advanced level, a new extended project** will allow the most able students to demonstrate high scholastic ability.

- **Extended schools** (see later section).

- **More personalised learning** (see later section).

More information on *Higher Standards, Better Schools for All* can be found at www.dfes.gov.uk/publications/schoolswhitepaper.

Extended schools

In many parts of the country, extended schools are already operating, but it is intended that schools will become much more central in providing a wide range of services to children, parents and the community. The government intends to spend £680 million by 2008 to facilitate these developments. Ideally these services should include:

- all-year childcare from 8.00am to 6.00pm

- referral to a wide range of support services, such as speech therapy, mental health and behaviour support

- exciting activities, including study support and extension/enrichment activities that will motivate the most able

- parenting support, which might include classes on healthy eating, helping children with homework, dealing with challenging behaviour etc

- community use of school facilities, especially ICT.

Again, this is an initiative that will benefit all children, especially those whose carers work. However, there are particular benefits for those children whose school performance suffers because they have nowhere to study at home and for those with talents that parents cannot nurture because of limited means.

More information on Extended Schools can be found at www.teachernet. gov.uk/settingup and www.tda.gov.uk/remodelling/extendedschools.aspx.

Personalised learning

As mentioned earlier in this chapter, a key component of current education reforms is the emphasis on personalised learning – maximising potential by tailoring education to individual needs, strengths and interests. The key features of personalised learning are:

- **Assessment for Learning** – Information from data and the tasks and assessments pupils undertake must be used to feed back suggestions about how work could be improved and what learning they need to do next. But the feedback should be a two-way process with pupils also providing information to teachers about factors impeding their learning and approaches that would enhance it. This feedback should inform future lesson planning. For the most able pupils, effective assessment for learning should mean that they move forward with their learning at an appropriate pace and depth, rather than marking time while others catch up.

- **Effective Teaching and Learning Strategies** – It is still the case that many teachers teach only in the way that was most successful for them as learners. There is ample evidence that our most able pupils do not form an homogeneous group and that, in order to bring out their many and varied gifts and talents, we need to adopt a wide range of teaching strategies, making full use of the opportunities provided by ICT. At the same time pupils need to become aware of the learning strategies that are most successful for them, whilst also exploring a broader range of learning approaches.

- **Curriculum Entitlement and Choice** – There are many examples of highly gifted adults whose abilities were masked at school because the curriculum did not appear to be relevant to them. Schools need to take the opportunities afforded by new flexibility in the curriculum, by the specialised diplomas of study being introduced for 14- to 19-year-olds and by partnership with other schools, colleges and businesses to engage their pupils. There are several schools now where more able pupils cover Key Stage 3 in two years. The year that is freed up by this approach can be used in a variety of ways, such as starting GCSE courses early, following an enrichment programme or taking up additional science and language courses. The possibilities are endless if there is desire for change.

- **School Organisation** – Effective personalisation demands a more flexible approach to school organisation. This flexibility might show itself in the way teaching and support staff are deployed, by the way pupils are grouped, by the structure of the school day and by the way in which ICT is used to enable learning to take place beyond the classroom. At least one school is abandoning grouping by age in favour of grouping by ability in the hope that this will provide the necessary challenge for the most able. It remains to be seen how successful this approach is but experimentation and risk-taking is essential if we are to make schooling relevant and exciting for our most able pupils.

- **Partnerships Beyond Schools** – Schools cannot provide adequately for their most able pupils without making full use of the opportunities and expertise offered by other groups within the community, including parents together with family support groups, social and health services, sports clubs and other recreational and business organisations.

The websites www.standards.dfes.gov.uk/personalisedlearning and www.teacher net.gov.uk/publications/ will provide more information on personalised learning, whilst new curriculum opportunities to be offered to 14- to 19-year-olds are described in www.dfes.gov.uk/14-19.

Self-evaluation and inspection

The most able must have as many opportunities for development as other pupils. Poor, unchallenging teaching or an ideology that confuses equality of opportunity with levelling down should not hinder their progress. They should have a fair share of a school's resources both in terms of learning materials and in human resources. The environment for learning should be one in which it is safe to be clever and to excel. These are points that schools should consider when preparing their self-evaluation and school development plans.

There have been dramatic changes in the relationships between schools and local authorities and in the schools' inspection regime since the Children Act 2004. Local authorities are now regarded as commissioners for services for children. One of their tasks is to facilitate the appointment of SIPs, School Improvement Partners, who act as the main conduit between schools and LAs and take part in an 'annual conversation' with their schools when the school's self-evaluation and progress towards targets is discussed.

Self-evaluation is also the cornerstone of the new shorter, more frequent Ofsted inspections, using a SEF (self-evaluation form) as a central point of reference together with the five outcomes for children of *Every Child Matters*. An invaluable tool for schools recognising that they need to do more for their gifted and talented pupils, or simply wanting to assess their current provision, is the institutional quality standards for gifted and talented education (IQS).

Institutional quality standards for gifted and talented education (IQS)

These standards, developed by a partnership of the DfES, NAGTY and other interested groups, are an essential self-evaluation tool for any school focusing on its gifted and talented provision. Under each of five headings, schools look carefully at the level indicators and decide which of the three levels they have achieved:

- **Entry level** – a school making its first steps towards developing a whole school policy might find that much of its provision falls into this category. Ofsted would rate such provision satisfactory.

- **Developing level** – where there is some effective practice but there is room for development and improvement. This aligns with a good from Ofsted.

- **Exemplary level** – where good practice is exceptional and sustained. Ofsted would rate this excellent.

The five headings show clear links to the personalisation agenda: effective teaching and learning strategies; enabling curriculum entitlement and choice; assessment for learning; school organisation; and strong partnerships beyond school.

Having identified the levels at which they are performing, schools are then able to draw up development plans. A copy of these standards is included in the appendices and more information about them can be found at www2.teachernet.gov.uk/qualitystandards.

Resources for teachers and parents of more able pupils

There is currently an abundance of resources and support agencies for teachers, parents and gifted and talented young people themselves. A few of general interest are included below. Other science examples will be found in later chapters of this book.

World Class Tests

These have been introduced by QCA to allow schools to judge the performance of their most able pupils against national and international standards. Currently tests are available for 9- and 13-year-olds in mathematics and problem solving. Some schools have found that the problem solving tests are effective at identifying able underachievers in maths and science. The website contains sample questions so that teachers, parents and pupils themselves can assess the tests' suitability for particular pupils or groups of pupils, and the tests themselves are also available online. For more information go to www.worldclassarena.org.uk.

National Curriculum Online

This website, administered by QCA, provides general guidance on all aspects of the National Curriculum but also has a substantial section on general and subject-specific issues relating to gifted and talented education, including identification strategies, case studies, management and units of work. Details of the National Curriculum Online can be found at www.nc.uk.net/gt.

G&TWise

G&TWise links to recommended resources for gifted and talented pupils, checked by professionally qualified subject editors, in all subjects and at all key stages and provides up-to-date information for teachers on gifted and talented education. Details can be found at www2.teachernet.gov.uk.

NACE – the National Association for Able Children in Education

NACE is an independent organisation that offers support for teachers and other professionals trying to develop provision for gifted and talented pupils. It gives advice and guidance to teachers and others, runs courses and conferences, provides consultants and keynote speakers.

It has also produced the NACE Challenge Award Framework, which it recommends could be used alongside IQS, as it exemplifies evidence and action planning. While IQS indicates what needs to be improved, the Challenge Award Framework suggests how to effect change. More information can be found at www.nace.co.uk.

National Association for Gifted Children (NAGC)

NAGC is a charity providing support for gifted and talented children and young people and their parents and teachers. It has a regional structure and in some parts of the country there are branch activities for children and parents. NAGC provides: counselling for both young people and their parents; INSET and courses for teachers; publications; activities for 3- to 10-year-olds; and a dedicated area on their website for 11- to 19-year-olds (to which they have exclusive access), called Youth Agency. For further information go to www.nagcbritain.org.uk.

Children of High Intelligence (CHI)

CHI acts on behalf of children whose intelligence puts them above the 98th percentile. It often acts in a support capacity when parents are negotiating appropriate provision with schools and local authorities. For further details visit www.chi-charity.org.uk.

Summary

- Schools must provide suitable challenge and support for their most able pupils.
- Appropriate provision can enhance motivation and improve behaviour.
- Recent legislation to support disadvantaged children should mean that fewer potentially gifted and talented children fall through the net.
- Effective self-evaluation of school provision for gifted and talented pupils and challenging targets are the keys to progress.
- There are many agencies that can help teachers with this work.

Departmental policy and approach

- Role of the subject/department leader
- Department policy
- Auditing provision
- Organisational strategies
- Links with other departments
- Developing literacy
- Developing cultural activities
- Monitoring individual learning plans
- Assessment
- INSET activities

In considering an approach to the education of our most gifted science students, it is worth noting that these pupils may experience needs alongside their strengths. Awareness and understanding of these needs is a key factor in helping such pupils to fulfil their potential. These pupils may find themselves experiencing a range of difficulties:

- **Isolation** from their peers as a result of their strengths or as a result of being seen to be different. In addition, pupils may feel isolated in their skill. It is important for both enjoyment and development for pupils to meet their like-minded peers and/or mentors.

- In the face of **adverse peer pressure**, pupils may feel self-conscious about their strengths, particularly within cultures where differences, gifts and talents are not celebrated or encouraged. The learning culture must be developed and pupils need to know that creative styles of work are valued and accepted. Peer pressure is often such that pupils are reluctant to differ from the majority for fear of rejection.

- **Unchallenged** gifted or talented pupils may exhibit adverse reactions. These can be of an emotional or behavioural nature or exhibited through limited or poor work.

- **Unidentified** gifted or talented pupils may suffer from frustration and/or low self-esteem. This can be masked by challenging or inappropriate behaviour, which often results in significant underachievement.

- Pupils who experience a **mismatch between their emotional understanding and intellectual development** may struggle with the social expectations placed upon them. Their emotional responses and social interaction skills may be at odds with what they are capable of academically. So, whilst perhaps the most academically able within a class, a pupil could potentially also be one of the least mature class members and experience significant difficulty with basic social interactions. This can lead to clashes due to misinterpretation of behaviour.

- **Parental pressure** can be a burden and source of worry to gifted and talented pupils. Parents need to be aware of the all-round needs of their child and to be helped and guided as to how best to foster their child's strengths. Schools have an important role in providing such guidance and may act as a link between parents and supportive organisations such as NAGC (National Association for Gifted Children).

- **Being valued for themselves** and not just for their abilities is essential for the emotional well-being of gifted and talented pupils.

The education of gifted students is the responsibility of all teachers, within all departments of the school, including the pastoral and senior management team. It can not be done solely by the school coordinator.

Role of subject/department leader

National standards have been developed for the subject leader for science so as to:

- set out clear expectations for the subject leader

- help plan and monitor their development, training and performance effectively, and to set clear, relevant targets for improving their effectiveness

- ensure that the focus at every point is on improving the achievement of pupils and the quality of their education

- provide a basis for the professional recognition of teachers' expertise and achievements

- help providers of professional development to plan and provide high quality, relevant training which meets the needs of individual teachers, makes good use of their time and has the maximum benefit for pupils.

The core purpose of the subject leader for science is to provide the professional leadership and management that will secure high quality teaching, effective use of resources and improved standards of learning and achievement for all pupils. For a detailed account the reader should refer to the *National Standards for Subject Leaders*, which are outlined on the DfES Standards website (www.standards.dfes.gov.uk/secondary/keystage3/respub/scienceframework/raising_standards/subject_leader/). In this section we will consider those aspects of the National Standards that relate specifically rather than generically to gifted science students.

Who is responsible?

As subject leader for science you are the lead professional in your department and you should lead the professional development of your staff so that they are fully able to identify, teach, monitor and evaluate the performance of your gifted science students. In this respect you should be fully aware yourself of all these attributes too. You should be able to give advice, support and direction to staff so that they feel confident in carrying out their duties within the department that you lead. Therefore, it is worthwhile ensuring that you have a good working relationship with the school coordinator for gifted and talented pupils. They will have a wealth of knowledge and experience that you can access. It is also worthwhile building up a bank of resources for when you are faced with questions from your staff. Listed below are a number of websites that will offer information on challenging able pupils in science:

- www.qca.org.uk for schemes, identification and case studies
- www.standards.dfes.gov.uk/excellence/gift for identification methods
- www2.teachernet.gov.uk/gat/ for subject-specific resources
- www.nace.co.uk for guidance and support
- www.nc.uk.net/gt/ for subject guidance
- www.ase.org.uk for technical and academic science support
- www.sciam.com for the latest science news
- www.scienceacross.com for an exchange of science reports.

You should endeavour to build on this list and also to encourage staff to add to the list.

Training for staff, including initial teacher training (ITT) students, newly qualified teachers and new members of the department, is essential to ensure effective delivery of challenging work for your most able students. You should aim to keep a list of high quality training providers, which may include the LA advisers, secondary strategy managers and lead professionals from local schools who have demonstrated expertise in this field for your subject. National organisations such as NACE are also able to offer training and publications to support you.

While you will be responsible as subject leader for all aspects of the education of more able pupils, you should consider delegating the tasks to a specific person within your department. Sometimes it may be appropriate for the departmental SEN representative to take on the role as coordinator for able pupils in science. Whoever the person may be, it should be noted that the subject leader remains responsible for the performance of these pupils.

Draft job description

The person with responsibility for more able pupils within the science department should manage the following areas:

- developing and implementing a policy for the effective education of the most able science students

- identification of able pupils

- matching the schemes of work to the needs of the able pupils

- providing guidance on teaching and learning methods to meet the needs of the most able

- setting challenging targets for pupils and staff

- monitoring achievement and underachievement, and have systems in place to act on both

- evaluating provision and attainment and using this information to help with subsequent planning for improvement

- continuing professional development for all staff

- developing effective links with other schools, the local community, business and industry in order to extend the science curriculum, enhance teaching and learning, and develop pupils' wider understanding.

Department policy

The purpose of a departmental policy for gifted and talented students is to ensure effective provision for this group. A departmental policy must be in line with the whole-school policy and support and implement its aims, and operate every day in the classroom. If implemented effectively, the policy should create a culture of sharing the values that support the education of able students within the department, and create a culture of coordinated, shared approaches to the teaching and development of able students.

The following checklist of points should be considered when designing a policy for the science department:

- aims of the policy
- identification strategies
- transition, transfer, processing and sharing of data
- provision in the scheme of work
- provision of resources
- differentiation
- variety of teaching and learning strategies
- extension and enrichment activities
- setting or grouping
- target-setting
- mentoring
- monitoring
- staff training and responsibilities
- parental involvement
- extracurricular activities
- cross-curricular links
- role of the teaching assistant.

In designing the departmental policy, the subject leader should consider how science contributes to the students' whole academic and personal development. It should identify areas that are not being fully developed elsewhere in the curriculum, but are part and parcel of their science education. It should be remembered that, in supporting the whole-school policy, the department has a duty to provide for all gifted and talented pupils within the school. Therefore, pupils who are gifted in maths or history or talented in music or sport will be in the cohort of students for whom provision is made. The department should not seek only to develop the gifted science students.

A sample general science policy for gifted students is provided in Appendix 2.1, and on the accompanying website. You can include additional material and amend it to suit your department.

Auditing provision

Many schools will have used programmes to audit current provision within departments and across the school. School self-review:

- is based on collection of evidence from a range of sources
- involves making judgements based on the interpretation and evaluation of data and evidence

- looks closely at the quality of teaching; pupils' attainment, achievement and progress; and leadership and management

- identifies effective practice

- examines what pupils know, understand and can do (impact)

- identifies strengths and weaknesses

- looks at trends over time

- has no point unless action follows the process.

The High Sights self-review programme was written by teachers from a group of Liverpool secondary schools and staff from the LA. A number of authorities across the country have adopted the programme. It considers seven areas of provision:

- How high are standards?

- How well are pupils' personal qualities developed?

- How effective are teaching and learning?

- How well does the curriculum meet pupils' needs?

- How well are pupils guided and supported?

- How effectively does the department work with parents and the community?

- How well is the department led and managed?

Some schools have used the subject audit that accompanies the Key Stage 3 National Strategy. The audit included as Appendix 2.2 (and on the accompanying website) uses some of the strategies from that document but also includes others that relate directly to provision for the most able. It helps staff to consider:

- the composition of the more able cohort in each year group

- current levels of attainment

- comparative levels of attainment

- the take-up of science at GCSE level and post-16

- pupils' attitudes to science

- departmental progress in developing provision for the most able

- extracurricular support.

Appendix 2.3 can be used to develop the departmental action plan for improving provision for the most able.

Monitoring provision

Monitoring provision should be done either by the head of department or the person responsible for gifted and talented pupils within the department. The method by which provision is monitored will differ from school to school and should ideally fit in with the existing processes for monitoring within the department. The following checklist is designed to get the monitoring process started:

- Check scheme of work for extension, enrichment and additional challenging activities.

- Check lesson plans for those activities and identified pupils.

- Observe lessons for appropriate challenge.

- Check students' work for evidence of challenging activities.

- Check students' work for independent learning.

- Creative thinking skills encouraged. How?

- Monitor test scores and targets.

- Request feedback from parents and students.

The departmental action plan (see the pro forma in Appendix 2.3 and on the website) will allow you to record priorities identified from the departmental audit. It is possible to plan when, who and how the targets set for improvement should be met, along with success criteria. Included on the action plan is space to record any resources required to achieve the targets set.

Example – Monitoring provision

The science department of a secondary school decided to evaluate the impact of its policy for gifted and talented students. The person with responsibility for the policy designed a questionnaire to give to pupils and parents. The pupils were asked to sit down with parents to complete the questionnaire, which comprised questions such as:

What are your favourite science topics? Which science topics do you enjoy least?

Which topics do you find easy, difficult, challenging, frustrating? Try to explain why.

How do you learn best? Which teaching style suits you?

Describe ways in which your teachers have enabled you to learn topics in depth.

What ways do you help yourself to learn more?

What more can we do to help you learn?

What are your own goals? What are you doing to achieve them? How can we help?

Teachers within the department were asked to identify students in each year group who were showing signs of excellence within their science lessons, as well as pupils from the identified cohort, so they could complete the questionnaire.

The results were used to check on the impact of the policy. The results also identified areas for development, which could be included in the policy on review.

Organisational strategies

Grouping policy

When deciding how to group gifted science students you have to remember that there is no correct way. There may be one that suits your school, your department, your staff or your pupils. The question should thus really be 'Which method of grouping will have most impact on our most able science students?' School timetable constraints may restrict certain models of grouping, such as setting in Year 7 or having subject specialists with top set Year 9 classes. Staffing problems may mean that you do not have a physics specialist spare to accelerate Year 9 pupils for GCSE, or one who is sufficiently knowledgeable for the task. We will thus consider a range of models and hope that elements of one or more may be suitable in your school.

Mixed ability groups

Many teachers will argue that teaching gifted students in mixed ability groups is impossible. However, children in Year 7 may feel that they want to stay with their tutor group while they settle in. We have to consider the pastoral issues and support the emotional development of the child. For this model to be successful there are certain things that teachers must do:

- differentiate effectively

- create a learning culture

- create a positive learning environment

- ensure all pupils feel valued.

The opportunity for coaching of less able by more able students presents itself here. All children bring their own particular abilities to a classroom environment and so all children may benefit. Can a gifted student really be taught in a mixed ability class? Let's look at a case study of how it could be put into practice.

Example – Providing for able pupils in a mixed ability setting

A Year 7 mixed ability science class was learning how to use a Bunsen burner at the start of autumn term. The teacher arranged the class into ability groups for the practical exercise. All children were given the instructions to follow for setting up, lighting and changing the Bunsen flame. Most were told to describe how the Bunsen flame changed and to work out how to test which flame was hottest. A small group was asked to examine the reasons behind the design of the Bunsen burner, when it would be appropriate to use the different flames, and what other uses were there for the different-coloured flames. The small group was asked to make a presentation of their findings during the next lesson. Two students who had simply practised lighting the Bunsen burner were asked to help demonstrate with the group because they were adept at speaking to an audience and liked to be hands-on. Two students from the middle group were asked to demonstrate how using the different flames to heat water could be timed to show their different temperatures.

The role of the teaching assistant (TA) is to support learners within the classroom. They should be available to support both the less able and the more able. The TA may also withdraw the gifted science students so as to focus on more challenging work or a more challenging practical activity.

For example, the students may be withdrawn and join a Year 9 class who are studying incomplete combustion. With the support of the TA the students can take part in the lesson and apply their learning at a higher level.

Setting

The practice of setting requires less preparation on the part of the teacher but differentiation is still necessary. The top set often has the widest ability range, from the exceptionally gifted science student to the steady plodder. The definition of a gifted and talented cohort is the top 10% of the school population in each year band. In a school with 180 students in each year, this would mean that 18 were on the cohort. However, this does not necessarily mean that they are all gifted scientists. Add to this the fact that a class would usually consist of around 30 pupils and you can see that the top set is not all your gifted students. Furthermore, there are various learning styles within the room, with visual, auditory and kinaesthetic learners each needing their own teaching strategy. The need for differentiation is thus obvious. Some schools have identified the learning styles of all their students, who then carry a card with them that flags up that learning style.

It would make sense then to have quite small top sets, with maybe 15–20 students. That is what happens with less able students because they require additional support. The gifted science students need as much guidance and support to extend them as far as possible. This would also facilitate fast tracking at each Key Stage.

Acceleration

Acceleration in this context is the advancement of a pupil beyond their chronological age. For example, a student who is identified as gifted in Year 7 may be moved into Year 9 to allow them to prepare for their SATs early. This form of organisation should only be used when:

- a pupil is in the top 2% of ability, i.e. consistently working at two National Curriculum Levels above average for his/her age in a range of subjects
- all stakeholders, including the child, parents, teachers and support staff, believe it to be in the best interests of the child
- a pupil is exceptionally mature, both socially and physically for their age
- it is not being considered under pressure.

Fast tracking

When students arrive in Year 7, they need to know that they are not simply going to revisit all the work they did in preparation for Key Stage 2 SATs. It is the duty of all science teachers to be aware of the science curriculum in the previous Key Stage. Without this information, teachers are assuming the student does not yet know this work or has been taught badly. This can have a negative impact on the pupil–teacher relationship, especially if the student is very knowledgeable or was taught by an inspirational teacher. Here are the QCA units for years 5–9:

Year 5

5A Keeping healthy | 5B Life cycles
5C Gases around us | 5D Changing state
5E Earth, moon and sun | 5F Changing sounds

Year 6

6A Interdependence and adaptation | 6B Micro-organisms
6C Dissolving | 6D Reversible and irreversible changes
6E Forces in motion | 6F How we see things
6G Changing circuits | 6H Solving problems

Year 7

7A Cells | 7B Reproduction
7C Environment and feeding relations | 7D Variation and classification
7E Acids and alkalis | 7F Simple chemical reactions
7G Solids, liquids and gases | 7H Solutions
7I Energy resources | 7J Electrical circuits
7K Forces and effects | 7L Solar system

Year 8

8A Food and digestion | 8B Respiration
8C Microbes | 8D Ecological relationships
8E Atoms and elements | 8F Compounds and mixtures
8G Rocks and weathering | 8H Rock cycle
8I Heating and cooling | 8J Magnets and electromagnets
8K Light | 8L Sound

Year 9

9A Inheritance and selection | 9B Fit and healthy
9C Plants and photosynthesis | 9D Plants for food
9E Reactions of metals and metal compounds | 9F Patterns of reactivity
9G Environmental chemistry | 9H Using chemistry
9I Energy and electricity | 9J Gravity and space
9K Speeding up | 9L Pressure and moments

When looking at these units it becomes clear that there is a great deal of overlap at the transition between Key Stages 2 and 3. How many times do we teach the students in Year 7 about the arrangement of particles in solids, liquids and gases (unit 7G)? The ideas are covered in Year 5, in unit 5C. Why do we teach students about dissolving (unit 7H) when it is covered in Year 6 (unit 6C)? Compacting or compressing the curriculum for the most able students allows them to move on to more difficult concepts and ideas that have not yet been covered.

Compacted curriculum at Key Stage 3 for early SATs entry

This is an example of how your most able students may be able to study for SATs, ready for assessment at the end of Year 8.

Example – Compacting the science curriculum

Year 7:

Units 7A, 7B, 8A, 8B for the biology units.

Units 7E, 8F, 8G, 8H for the chemistry units.

Units 7J, 8I, 8J and a combined 8K/8L unit for the physics units.

Key learning points from the discarded units should be put into a formal assessment at the end of Year 7. The students should be told that they will be assessed on these key learning points and a revision sheet given. The assessment should be used to identify any weaknesses in the students' knowledge about those units so that intervention strategies can be put into place at the end of the summer term or over the summer holiday. This could be in the form of a summer school or holiday homework assignments.

Year 8:

Units 9A (plus elements from 7D), 9B (plus elements from 8C), 9C, 9D for the biology units.

Units 9E, 9F, 9G (plus elements from 7C and 8D), 9H for the chemistry units.

Units 9J (plus elements from 7L), 9K, 9L (plus elements from 7K) for the physics units.

This model may not suit your department but it can be used as a starting point and altered to fit your staffing capabilities, available resources and suitability of your gifted science students.

Students may be entered early for SATs in Year 8. They may then embark upon a GCSE course to keep the momentum going. The advantage of this is to stimulate the gifted students and they can focus solely on GCSE work during Year 9.

Compressing the curriculum at Key Stage 3 for GCSE entry.

An alternative to the above model is to match units in Year 9 with GCSE units from Years 10 or 11. The students do not follow a compacted curriculum in Years 7 and 8, and study the Year 9 units as they should. However, the additional required information is added to Year 9 units to allow students to sit modular GCSE exams during Year 9. They may enter the SATs exams at the normal time.

Case study

After discussions with the school leadership group, the head of a large science department introduced GCSE units alongside the normal course of study for Year 9 pupils. It was piloted with just one group, the top set. The department had recently switched to a modular science course and had found it suited the children at the school.

In Year 9, students studying unit 9A followed the scheme of work from the GCSE unit called 'Inheritance and survival'. They then sat a 20 minute multiple choice exam in November. After Christmas they studied unit 9H, following the GCSE scheme of work from the unit called 'Chemistry in action'. This was followed by a multiple choice exam in March. Finally, they studied unit 9I, following the scheme of work for the GCSE unit 'Energy and electricity'. The students did their SATs exams in May as usual, and then completed a third modular multiple choice exam at the end of May. All the other units were studied as usual.

The students felt motivated and challenged by the pilot. They went on to complete their GCSE modules, coursework and terminal exam at the end of Year 10. The results for the science department were improved also because the students could go on to study additional science GCSE subjects.

Compressing the curriculum at Key Stage 4

While the government recommends that all students should study dual science, it is only a recommendation. Schools do not have to force students to study dual science and if the school has specialist college status it may even encourage them into single science. Schools that have been successful in gaining language college status may want their students at Key Stage 4 to study at least two languages. Specialist sports colleges may want their students to opt for double PE. Technology colleges may encourage their students to do double ICT. So what do you do if you have lots of students opting for single science, many of whom were your gifted scientists in Year 9?

The science department clearly needs to differentiate for this group and to follow the usual strategies for supporting able children in the classroom. However, these choices can have repercussions later in the child's school career, such as not being able to select a science A level.

Example – Compacting the curriculum at KS4

After a secondary school had gained sports college status, the science department found that the number of pupils selecting dual science fell from over 100 to around 30 students. Many students chose to do double PE or ICT instead. The head of department consulted schools locally and the LA effectiveness officer. The solution was to fast track the single award. Students completed their coursework at the end of Year 9. Modular exams were completed in November, March and May of Year 10 after students rotated around the subject specialists in the department. The terminal exam was done in June of Year 10.

When results came out in the summer, students were grouped into either a re-sit class if the grade was below the target grade, a GCSE biology separate science class or a GCSE astronomy class. Students who had not chosen dual science, but were highly able or gifted, were still given the chance to complete two GCSE science courses. This led to a larger than usual A level class the following year for biology.

Allocation of resources

It is important that the most able get a fair share. If there are a limited number of specialist science rooms, their use should be rotated so that all pupils have access to these resources. There may be a temptation to spend on books and other resources that cater for middle range and lower ability range. Schools must provide for the most able too, at least giving parity with SEN provision.

Links with other departments

Remember that your most able students in science may be gifted in other subjects too. However, it is unlikely that you will find many students who are evenly gifted in science and a range of other subjects. Researchers such as Achter *et al.* (1997) have found that there is a considerable amount of unevenness between abilities in the different intelligence domains. A parity in abilities in maths and languages was found to be the exception rather than the rule. They researched 1,000 gifted students and found that 95% of them showed considerable differences between their abilities in maths and languages. So if only 5% were found to have comparable levels of ability in maths and languages, then this gives us some indication of the chances of having a gifted science student who is also equally gifted in a range of other subjects.

After identifying your own cohort of able students in science you should consult with the school coordinator and compare the students on the school cohort with those you have identified:

- Which students are common to the school cohort?

- Are any students listed as able in a range of subjects?

- Are any students listed as able in one or two other subjects?

- Are any of the students that you identified not found on the school cohort?

Students identified as able in a range of subjects.

Students that are identified as being able in a range of subjects are going to be few and far between. It should be assumed that these students will be working closely will the school coordinator and will be familiar with a range of teaching and learning strategies. They may be called upon by many different departments to take part in out-of-school activities, concerts, competitions and enrichment activities. Additional to this they may have a range of personal interests that they are involved in out of school – horse riding, basketball, judo, astronomy.

All of these activities place a huge demand on the individual and so it makes sense to coordinate the work being done by the broadly able student. This should be done by the school coordinator, but the responsibility also rests with the science teacher to ensure that these students receive a challenging learning environment in terms of education rather than time management.

Each school will have its own method of recording homework, e.g. homework diaries, planners, etc. The responsibility is on each teacher to ensure they stick to the school homework timetable so as not to overload the able student. It is worthwhile getting to know the interests of these students – clubs, music, sports – so as to plan around them.

Consultation with other heads of department can:

- enlighten you about unknown interests and strengths of the broadly able student

- offer an opportunity to negotiate the time available after school or at lunchtime to organise clubs, rehearsals and activities

- allow sharing of data and attainment

- encourage sharing of concerns on attainment or behaviour

- encourage sharing teaching and learning strategies that have been successful

- help to monitor the range of learning opportunities being offered

- allow sharing of examples of good practice.

Case study

A school wanted to ensure that the number of students in Year 9 achieving Levels 7 and 8 in their English, maths and science SATs increased. To help with the coordination of revision lessons, the deputy head teacher arranged a meeting between the heads and Key Stage coordinators of English, maths and science. This meeting took place at the end of January, with the SATs scheduled for the beginning of May. At that meeting it was agreed that the targeted pupils, capable of achieving at the highest levels, would be named and this information collated by the deputy head, with the assistance of the school coordinator for able students.

Staff present discussed individual pupils, their attainment so far, their chances of achieving at the highest levels, planned strategies for revision lessons, requirements for the revision lessons, and concerns about individual students. Students for whom English was an additional language were identified so that a reader could be found to read and also translate words or groups of words within the SATs questions. Each department then negotiated the day on which after-school classes would take place.

As the classes were coordinated centrally, the pressure on the students was reduced because the students did not have to choose between subjects. Information and materials were provided for the students, with a revision schedule that included dates for other commitments such as sport and music. This time spent planning in advance was also of great benefit to staff in ensuring that students had ample opportunity to revise higher level work and questions.

Students identified as able in one or two subjects

More frequently you will find students who are able in both science and other subjects such as maths or geography. This is because either the subject material is similar or the thinking processes required to access the subjects are similar.

The benefits in liaising with other departments are the same as listed in the previous section. However, it can be easier working with only one or two other departments rather than several for the following reasons:

- more frequent liaison

- opportunity to share resources

- targeted activities in class

- sharing of out-of-school activities

- shared teaching expertise to cover shared topics.

Case study

A science department and a geography department decided to work together to encourage their most able students. After looking at their subject cohorts of able students in Year 9 they found that 12 students were on both subjects' lists. The Key Stage 3 coordinators worked together to identify areas in the schemes of work that would best enrich and extend this group of students. It was decided that a weekend activity trip to study rocks and rock formations would be suitable. The site chosen to visit was a disused tin mine. For the geography department the focus was on different rock formations and how they were formed, mining and materials, and leisure and tourism. For the science department the focus was on materials from mining, including metals. The following questions were posed to the students to encourage higher order thinking skills:

- Are the earth's resources finite? What does this mean for the mining industry? What does this mean for the manufacturing industry? How will consumers be affected? (questions focusing on application)

- Choose a metal that is mined. What is the best method of extraction found so far? How would life be different if supplies of that metal became exhausted? What substitute materials could be used? Explain their limitations. (questions focusing on analysis)

- What is the most effective way of increasing the lifetime of finite materials? Who is responsible for ensuring that an appropriate rate of extraction is achieved? What role do we as individuals play in ensuring the future of finite materials? (questions focusing on synthesis and evaluation)

One member of staff from each department accompanied the students. The group comprised 20 students. There were 12 from the shared cohort plus 8 who were agreed upon by both departments as able students that would benefit from the enrichment and extension activity. All students had to complete an orientation worksheet prior to leaving which gave factual information about the tin mining industry, as well as the mining of other metals commonly used by consumers.

The questions posed to students on the day of the activity had to be presented in the form of a newspaper, with news, interviews, factual stories and adverts for products using the materials explored. The newspapers were used in lessons on their return for critical analysis by all the students in the science class and the geography class. The articles were critically examined for consequences, assumptions, main issues, prejudice, evidence and examples, and reliability and relevance. This taught all the students to think critically about what they read.

Students identified as able in science only

It would seem on the face of it that the group of students identified as able in science only would be the easiest to cultivate and challenge. However, those that excel in the sciences may well not be the most literate, grammatical, creative or cultural students that you teach. Thus in order to develop a well-rounded able science student it is important to develop all these characteristics too.

Developing literacy

In order to promote literacy you may wish to consider using some of the strategies listed below:

Mnemonics

These examples were written by a Year 7 group at the start of the forces unit, to demonstrate prior learning:

- FORCES – friction on roads changes even speed.

- BALANCE – balance a lever and not change ends.

- SPEED – speed pushes everyone ever distant.

- UPTHRUST – under pressure the huge resultant upthrust squashes torpedoes.

Whilst the examples may not all be scientifically accurate, they offer an opportunity to discuss literacy in a scientific context. What words could be improved upon? How does tense affect the mnemonic? Which words are missing that would normally be required to make a proper sentence? Could punctuation help with meaning?

Comprehension

The students may be asked to answer questions or prepare a set of comprehension questions on a passage of text. The following passage was presented to a Year 10 GCSE student and she was asked to read it and prepare five questions that would encourage higher order thinking skills. The student was familiar with higher order thinking skills from her previous lessons and had some experience of answering such comprehension questions.

Herbicide

As a little boy I remember my older sister telling me that there were no such things as weeds. Only beautiful plants that are growing in a place that they are not meant to grow in. Hence, any plant, no matter how beautiful or rare, could be classified as a weed if the person observing it decided that it should not be there. This was very upsetting for me as I had also observed my mother preparing the weed killer the previous day. It had been a hot but windy day, and after mixing 3 caps full of the concentrated chemical liquid into a watering can labelled 'Herbicide', she filled the can with water from the garden tap up to the 1 gallon mark. My mother did not use the herbicide that day. I remember her looking up to the sky, tutting and then carrying the can to a safe corner of the garden where she left it, covered by a black polythene bag.

As my sister walked away my eyes were drawn to that corner of the garden. There my mother stood, her gloved hands clenching the handle of the can. As I turned away I could not help but think 'Is the beauty I see in each vibrant flower as well received by the holder of that floral pollutant?' Then, as she poured, nothing changed. I knew that it would be a slow undignified death for all that drank it.

After reading this text the student wrote the following questions:

- Why do gardeners use herbicides in their gardens?

- What alternatives could they use?

- What conditions affect the application of herbicides? Why?

- How could herbicides be improved?

- Draw up a checklist of factors to consider when deciding if a plant is a weed. Discuss how each may be interpreted by different gardeners.

Writing for a purpose

This type of literacy activity can encourage free writing and creativity. The form of the activity can be varied:

- Write a story – *the journey of an atom of aluminium from mining through to use and recycling.*

- Write a poem – *bring to life the story of the changes in rocks from magma to igneous then metamorphic rock.*

- Write a report – *write an article for the Times newspaper on the possible impact of GM foods on developing economies* or *evaluate the connection between the prescription of antibiotics and the rise in resistant infectious microorganisms.*

- Construct a dialogue – *what would the two atoms in a molecule of oxygen discuss as they passed into and through your body?*

- Correct a text. This activity can suit a student with lower literacy skills or a student with English as an additional language (EAL). The text is composed with deliberate errors. These errors may be scientific, grammatical, spelling or malapropism. The following text shows examples of all four types of error.

The student should be encouraged to identify and underline the error. Then they should write the correct word/sentence structure. The student could be asked to rewrite the passage with the corrections or improvements.

> Pollution is the continuation of one substance by some other so that the original substance can no longer be used for the purpose it was intended. We humans are polluting rivers, lakes, seas, air and the earth with gases and other chemicals. These parts of our environment have all been used as dispersal sites for unwanted substances.
>
> One example of pollution is the release of particular carbon from the burning of coal in power stations. This settles on plants and affects the leaf's ability to photosynthesise. One way of stopping pollution is to make laws which find people heavy if they are polluting regardless of the amount.

The reader may wish to turn to chapter 4 and read the section on developing thinking skills to get more information on teaching able students creative and critical thinking.

Developing cultural activities

For a variety of reasons, our schools are becoming more multicultural. By embracing all the cultures of the students within our schools we can benefit from a diverse range of experiences.

The government has also recognised that certain ethnic groups have been underachieving in our schools. This is a complex issue, but has led to changes in the way that those schools which are most ethnically diverse approach the teaching and learning of all of its students.

One initiative, the African-Caribbean Project, focused on the identification of students' ethnicity, targeting attainment and changing schemes of work to make them relevant to students from a range of African and Caribbean cultures. This latter point does not require a huge amount of work, just a little bit of updating to include different examples. There is an example of a scheme of work incorporating African-Caribbean culture on the accompanying website.

Certain units in Key Stage 3 are easily modified or updated to include additional examples. A brief list is shown on page 35 to demonstrate how easy it is to get started on improving the cultural education of your able science students.

Monitoring individual learning plans

Students should be encouraged to monitor their own work. The progress log provided on the accompanying website allows students to write down any additional challenging tasks set by staff. The log may be used generally for all science tasks, or may be designed to focus on differentiated homework activities. The advantages of using this form are as follows:

● encourages independent learning

● sets challenging targets

Unit	Title	Examples
7A	Cells	Compare red blood cells with sickle cells. Comparison of pollen grains across continents to map continental drift.
7C	Environment and feeding relationships	Food chains from African savannah, coral reefs from the Caribbean
7D	Classification and variation	Melanin production
7L	The solar system	Images from South African observatory
8A	Food and digestion	Food tests using papaya, cassava, couscous
8C	Microbes	AIDS epidemic in some African countries, malaria, tsetse fly, sleeping sickness
8D	Ecological relationships	African and Caribbean animals and plants
9A	Inheritance and selection	Link between sickle cell anaemia and malaria
9C	Plants and photosynthesis	Irrigation systems, wells and problems of soil erosion/humus content of soil
9D	Plants and food production	Global food production, vegetables imported from African countries
9I	Energy and electricity	HEP, solar power

Incorporating cultural awareness in science education

- assists in formulating a routine

- informs the monitoring process.

The progress log, when used and completed by the student, can also be used as a prompt sheet when discussing their individual learning plan (ILP). The progress log serves to remind the student of what tasks have been given, whether they have been completed, and what comments the teacher has made about their progress. A sample ILP is given as Appendix 2.4, and is included on the accompanying website. This is intended as a guide only and can be tailored to meet the needs of the individual school.

Time spent with the able student reviewing their progress is time well spent. So, err on the side of caution when deciding on the design of the ILP. If it is too detailed with many boxes to be filled, or with large boxes requiring detailed writing, then your time with the student will be spent doing just that – filling in boxes and writing. Also consider what you plan to do with the ILP. If it is to be used to inform planning of differentiated personalised learning then it needs to be referred to regularly. A large, unwieldy document is less likely to be referred to regularly if the information has to be read in depth before getting to the relevant parts. You may also wish to share the ILP with the student and parents/carers. With this in mind, a simplified pro forma is desirable.

There is much data available on pupils. You can include as much or as little as you wish. Whatever information you do include, make it precise – use sublevels or raw scores rather than Levels for attainment and targets. Make use of the data already provided for you. The Fisher Family Trust data that is provided by many authorities gives all the raw scores for Key Stage 2 SATs as well as sublevels. It also gives predictions on sublevel targets for Key Stage 3 English, maths and science, the chances of achieving those targets, and also the predictions for Key Stage 4 GCSE grades. It is important that the targets that you set for the students are shared with them.

It is also important that you share with the students the areas that you and your colleagues identify as strengths. You should encourage the students to know their strengths, giving them the opportunity to focus on them and to use them to their best advantage. There is then also the opportunity for students to put forward their own identified strengths – some of which staff may not have considered or noticed. This two-way dialogue helps to build the learning culture with the students.

Assessment

Assessment using evidence of higher order thinking

In Chapter 3 you will find a section on the identification of students and their characteristics. One of the characteristics is the ability to use higher order thinking skills of analysis, synthesis and evaluation from an early age. With this in mind, it is important to plan lessons that promote and have opportunities for the use of higher order thinking skills. You will recognise students using higher order thinking by:

- their thinking in an abstract fashion despite their young age

- their many questions, ones which suggest they are also willing to give opinions or predict outcomes

- the way they provide alternative strategies for practical investigations, or even alternative practical experiments to demonstrate the same point

- the provision of reasoned and credible explanations for phenomena

- the creativity in the way they present ideas and question other people's ideas

- the use and understanding of models, and the development of their own models to explain concepts

- the way they apply learning to new circumstances

- the ability to argue objectively by using a range of sources of evidence.

The challenge for us is to ensure that our students are provided with the opportunities in lessons to engage in higher order thinking skills. This can provide an assessment tool to monitor the students' performance.

One way of achieving this is the use of the 'big ideas' strategy. A section of a lesson is given over to thinking about some big ideas, then discussing them with peers. A case study is shown below.

Case study – 'Big ideas' with Year 8

A group of mixed ability, mixed gender Year 8 pupils in an inner city comprehensive were studying temperature and energy in unit 8I, Heating and Cooling. It was the second lesson on this topic and the teacher had completed about 30 minutes of the lesson. The teacher then wrote on the board 'Wherever you go on our planet there will always be some heat energy'. The students were asked to pair up and discuss this idea. The teaching assistant went around the room with some large Post-it notes, one per group. After 5 minutes the students were asked to record the outcome of their conversation. The Post-it notes were placed on a display board at the front of the class. The teacher grouped them according to responses, and then went through the notes in order of complexity.

- Four groups disagreed and pointed out that if you went in a freezer section of a supermarket there was no heat energy.

- One group said it would only be possible if you were locked inside a freezer.

- Three groups said that it depended on where you were in the world and that places like the South Pole had no heat energy.

- One group said that if you were outdoors anywhere in the world during the day then there was heat energy from the sun.

- One group said that from their work in Year 7 (unit 7G, Solids, liquids and gases) they remembered that all things were made from atoms, which moved because they have energy, and to change state they require more energy – this must mean that because there are solids, liquids and gases all over the world there is also heat energy everywhere.

The other students benefited from this enlightenment from previous learning, and the teacher also had a written record of assessment of the able students in the class.

It is not always possible to get a written record of responses. Sometimes it is useful to ask the classroom assistant to record responses given verbally by children.

Assessment using scientific investigation

In developing scientific enquiry skills in our students we are also providing challenging opportunities for our most able to use higher order thinking skills. The following table, adapted from Coates and Eyre (1999) and Coates and Wilson (2000), shows the links between attainment target 1 (AT1) and higher order thinking skills.

When using scientific enquiry (Sc1) to challenge your students, it is more productive to focus on part of an investigation, such as controlling variables, rather than the whole thing.

Higher level thinking outlined in Bloom's *Taxonomy of Educational Objectives* (1956)	Scientific enquiry (Sc1/AT1 Level 6)
Analysis	In their own investigative work, they (the children) use scientific knowledge and understanding to identify an appropriate approach.
Synthesis	Children draw conclusions that are consistent with the evidence and use scientific knowledge and understanding to explain them.
Evaluation	Children make reasoned suggestions about how their working methods could be improved.

Case study – Bone strength

A group of Year 9 students, studying unit 9B, Fit and healthy, wanted to investigate whether increasing the diameter of a bone also increased the strength. They were going to do this using paper tubes to represent the bone and hang more weights on the bone until it bent.

● All students identified the need to use the same weights to hang on the bone each time and to keep the thickness and length of paper the same. The only change was in the diameter of the bone.

● Some students identified the need to keep the rolled up paper in a circular shape for all diameters.

● One student identified that the width of the paper must vary to allow for the thickness of the paper to remain the same for each diameter. As the diameter increases so must the width of the paper, or the paper will be overlapping in the tube and create a thicker bone. However, the student also pointed out that he noticed (from the dinner table) that wider bones tended to be thicker and that the model was not accurate because the relationship between the diameter and the thickness of paper was not equal for each bone.

To complete a whole investigation requires children to plan, obtain and present evidence, consider the evidence and evaluate that evidence. If children always have to complete a full scientific enquiry they will become bored. This often leads to non-completion of the task and the students thus not attempting to evaluate the evidence and the process, which has the greatest potential for higher order thinking skills. Present evidence of the process and data obtained by other students, or from secondary sources, to allow them to reflect on improvement more often.

Remind students that it is not just about gaining knowledge and applying it. They need to understand that there is a process going on that can be applied to a range of subjects, and this is the focus of their learning. In the above example, the thickness of bone that was the strongest is not the learning outcome. The learning outcome is the ability to identify variables to control.

Using scientific enquiry to assess thinking

Many strands of the scientific enquiry process offer the chance to assess higher order thinking. Examples include predicting the outcome of changing variables, looking for patterns in data, and predicting the shape of a graph. This type of assessment requires little in the way of recording by the student, and so is a quick way for teachers to assess progress and attainment.

Case study – Boiling water

A group of Year 7 students were learning how to use the Bunsen burner. The teacher had set them the task of analysing an experiment done the previous year by a Year 7 class. The plan, with diagrams, was presented to the students, along with the recorded results of the experiment. The results showed the temperature of the water recorded every 1 minute for 10 minutes.

The students were asked to comment on the suitability of the plan. This gave the teacher the chance to talk about the process of setting up and using the Bunsen burner. The teacher then asked the students to identify and explain any patterns in the results. All students identified that the temperature of the water increased during the experiment, from 30°C to 80°C. Some students identified that the temperature had risen at roughly 5°C intervals, but the intervals were smaller at the hotter end. One student noted that the greater the temperature difference between the room and the water, the more energy was required to lift and maintain the temperature. Also, that the reading on the thermometer would fall more quickly if the measurement was taken by removing the thermometer from the water. The student asked if the method of reading the thermometer could be included in the plan. The teacher asked the student to write down her own ideas about improving the plan.

Links with other departments

There are a number of opportunities to investigate experimental evidence, check on data, identify areas for development in plans for experiments, and whether conclusions based on experimental evidence are valid. These can be used to make links with other departments through a range of cross-curricular activities. Listed below is a selection of ideas from the Year 9 scheme of work. Note also the use of relevant research that is regularly in the news.

You will come across assessment of scientific enquiry at GCSE. The coursework that students have to do can comprise 20% of their grade or more. If the students have been given learning opportunities at Key Stage 3 that allows them to analyse exemplar material critically, then they will be better prepared at GCSE for the coursework and so maximise attainment. The four strands of planning, observing, analysing and evaluating build on pupils' ability to think. Appendix 2.5 provides a writing frame that will allow students to complete their coursework effectively (this is also available on the website). The analysis and evaluation of their work is a higher order thinking skill. For ideas on general ways of building thinking skills into your lessons and developing these skills in students, refer to Chapter 4.

Unit	Title	Cross-curricular themes
9A	Inheritance and selection	• Research into the Human Genome Project and its impact on the spectre of designer babies, babies for organs, etc. [child development]
9B	Fit and healthy	• Validity of the Atkins diet. [PE] • Research the theory behind a specific training regime and its validity. [PE]
9C	Plants and photosynthesis	• Investigate what wavelengths of light are optimum for photosynthesis/sun spectra. [physics/biology]
9D	Plants for food	• Effect of different yeasts to make bread. [catering] • Investigate crop rotation in association with a local farm. [community]
9E	Reactions of metals and metal compounds	• Use of metal compounds in glass blowing. [art] • Properties of solder in relation to uses. [technology]
9F	Patterns of reactivity	• Look at the use of the Group 1 metal compounds in the manufacture of fireworks. [business studies]
9G	Environmental chemistry	• Produce a news article outlining a cost/benefit analysis for an environmental issue, such as the Kyoto agreement. [English/PSHE]
9H	Using chemistry	• How chemicals are extracted from plants and used in the manufacture of makeup, shampoo and soap. [chemistry]
9I	Energy and electricity	• Cost analysis for the electricity used in the school. [maths] • Design efficient electrical heating/lighting systems. [technology]
9J	Gravity and space	• History of space travel article. [history/English]
9K	Speeding up	• Big Bang versus Creation. [RE]
9L	Pressure and moments	• Investigate the suits worn by Olympic athletes to improve streamlining in air/water. [textiles] • Car streamlining. [local business]
9M	Investigating scientific questions	• Design a wheel brace. [maths/technology] • Investigate tyre pressure and fuel consumption. [maths] • Evaluate rocket design. [technology]

Links between departments

INSET activities

The type of INSET that you may want to provide within your department will depend on the experience of the staff and their willingness to undergo such training. On the accompanying website you will find a simple outline PowerPoint presentation that gives a brief summary of:

- definitions

- characteristics of a gifted science student

- barriers to identification

- identification tools

- policy

- classroom provision, with examples

- activities.

It is assumed that you will add to this outline using information pertinent to your school. This may include your own school-specific barriers to identification (for example, high EAL or large number of statements), departmental identification tools, your own policy, and an outline of the current activities undertaken by your able students.

Alongside this presentation, you may also wish to consider auditing learning styles and identifying the preferred learning styles within your departmental staff. Use this to generate discussion on how each member of the department teaches, and whether this has a positive or negative impact on pupils. This can be done quickly by using the preferred learning styles quick questionnaire, provided in Appendix 2.6 (and on the website).

From this you can lead on to the teaching styles and techniques analysis in Appendix 2.7 (and on the website), which will allow staff to consider not just how they teach, but also the evidence they could provide and include in the school evaluation form (SEF). This is an important tool, especially as school inspections rely ever more heavily on the SEF in preparation for inspection visits. The collection and collation of evidence will identify strengths and areas for development within each teacher's teaching repertoire and across the department as a whole.

Recognising high ability and potential

- Good practice in identification strategies
- What makes a gifted science student?
- Identification methods
- Identifying gifted pupils with EAL
- Identifying gifted pupils with low literacy levels
- Multiple intelligences and learning styles
- Case studies

Before we start this chapter, it may be useful to consider some interesting facts about learning:

- People learn in different ways – visual, auditory and kinaesthetic learning.

- Learning is greatly enhanced when the whole brain is engaged.

- People remember unexpected, dramatic, emotional experiences. They remember context more than content.

- Without review, information is quickly forgotten.

- Motivation is key to learning. People learn when they want to learn.

- The brain learns best when it is trying to make sense of something.

- Learning is greatest at the beginning and end, and less in the middle (BEM).

- Children can only concentrate for two minutes greater than their chronological age. In adults it is no more than 20–25 minutes.

- Low stress – high challenge encourages effective learning.

- The brain needs fuel. Oxygen, water, protein and rest are necessary for the brain to function efficiently.

Many of you will be familiar with the learning pyramid, devised by the National Training Laboratories (USA). It is worthwhile focusing on the learning pyramid whilst thinking about preparing for our most able student learners.

The Learning Pyramid

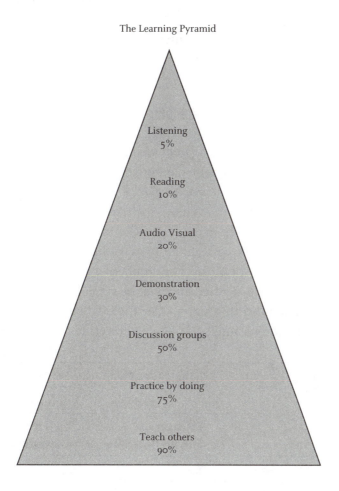

Student Recall Rate

Good practice in identification strategies

All schools must identify the top 10% of their students. These will be classified as the gifted and talented cohort. The gifted students include those who are most able in one or more of the statutory school curriculum subjects, such as science, and account for 7% of the cohort. The remaining 3% will be talented in art, design, music, PE or performing arts. It is up to each individual school to determine whether the cohort is made up of individuals who are gifted or talented in one or two subjects, or whether it is composed primarily of good all-rounders. This will obviously impact on the number of students who are on both the school cohort and the departmental cohort.

The identification strategies used must include a balance of hard data, such as the results of National Curriculum tests, and a wide range of qualitative evidence, including teacher assessment, nomination by peers/parents/staff, pupil observation and examination of pupils' work. The cohort should reflect high achievers and those who have the potential to achieve but are not regularly demonstrating high achievement (underachievers). The identification process is therefore continuous and needs to make provision for movement into and out of the cohort, especially as students may join your school at any time during the year.

Your department should ensure that the identification process is rigorous, transparent and fair. It should not discriminate against any particular group based on religion, gender, social class, or ethnicity.

What makes a gifted science student?

The table below lists some of the characteristics of a gifted science student. They may not all apply to all such students and other characteristics may not be shown – this is a simple guide. The table can be used to record the observations made by staff as part of the qualitative information gathered, and used in the identification process. The observed evidence may be answers to questions, whether written or verbal, practical activity or design, ability to make links or explain new ideas. The identification outcome may be a series of numbers from 1 to 7, where 4 is average ability, 5 is above average, 6 is gifted and 7 is the sign of a highly able student. The recording of information in this way makes the qualitative information used for identification more rigorous and is less likely to be criticised for subjectivity.

High ability checklist		
Pupil:	Teacher:	
Trait	**Observed evidence/date**	**Identification outcome**
Go beyond obvious answers		
Relate obscure facts		
Explain using models		
Dissatisfied with simple answers		
Miss out steps to problems		
Question others, even teachers		
Consider alternatives		
Spot patterns		
More extensive vocabulary		
Mathematical skills		
Bored by simple repetition		
Self-critical		
Careless with easy work		
Intense interest in one area		
Think logically, giving explanations for phenomena		

Identification methods

There is a range of quantitative data available in science, as it is a core subject:

- Key Stage 2 and 3 SATs Levels from QCA as well as teacher-assessed SATs Levels

- NfER, CAT, MiDYiS/YELLIS data for verbal, non-verbal and maths, if used in your school

- Fisher Family Trust data

- unit test scores/end-of-year exam scores

- attainment in scientific enquiry

- performance in modular science exams at Key Stage 4.

Wherever possible, the information gathered should be broken down into sublevels or raw scores as levels and grades are too broad. No one piece of information alone will reveal a gifted science pupil. It is necessary to build up a profile of a pupil with a full range of data and qualitative attributes.

It should also be noted that not all pupils perform well in written tests. One reason for this may be that the pupil has English as an Additional Language (EAL) and literacy skills are still developing.

Identifying gifted pupils with EAL

Pupils arriving as immigrants or refugees from Europe, North Africa, the Far East or Asian countries may not speak English at all, or have limited vocabulary. Reading, understanding questions and synthesising the expected responses may be difficult even if the pupil is gifted. Additionally, reliance on IQ tests alone can greatly reduce the potential number of gifted students. Renzulli (1978) indicated that 'more creative persons come from below the 95th percentile than above it, and if such cut-off scores are needed to determine entrance into special programs, we may be guilty of actually discriminating against persons who have the highest potential for high levels of accomplishment' (p. 182). A range of alternative assessment methods needs to be made available in order to give students several opportunities to demonstrate their skills, and to assess potential aptitude.

One such set of assessments are the Ravens Progressive Matrices. These are designed to assess a person's intellectual ability to make sense of complex data, to perceive and to think clearly. Each of the problems within the tests is presented as a sequence of symbols. The person being assessed is required to understand the relationship between the symbols and find the one symbol that completes the sequence. By doing so the person demonstrates their level of reasoning. The term 'progressive' refers to the fact that the problems in the test variants (they come in different forms) become progressively more difficult.

The benefits of using the Ravens Progressive Matrices are that:

- they can be used for all ability levels

- there are extensive norms for different ages and cultures

- they are easy to administer and score

- they overcome the cultural and language bias.

More information about these assessments, training and how to purchase them is available at www.testagency.com.

Non-verbal assessment strategies

- **Physical demonstration:** Students may be allowed to point or use other gestures to express academic concepts without speech. They can also be asked to perform hands-on tasks or to act out vocabulary, concepts or models.

- **Pictorials:** Students may be asked to produce or manipulate drawings, models, graphs and charts. For example, pictorial representations of oxygen, carbon dioxide, water, light, glucose can be labelled in the appropriate position on a plant to show understanding of photosynthesis.

- **Practical planning:** An idea may be presented to a student who then has to find ways of testing the idea. Cut-out diagrams can be given to allow the construction of a practical procedure, presented in order. A drawing may be presented to show predicted outcomes.

An alternative to using English language standardised tests is the use of assessment in the native language of the student. The standardised English language tests measure a variety of skills: creative thinking skills such as fluency, flexibility, originality and elaboration; intellectual development; language proficiency; and non-verbal perceptual skills of cognitive development. Students with EAL could not access these tests sufficiently to demonstrate proficiency in any of these skills, regardless of their ability in their home language.

Identifying gifted pupils with low literacy levels

Scientific enquiry and practical activities are obvious choices for the assessment of this group of pupils. The student may be offered a range of possible outcomes from an experiment, and they then have to comment on the validity of each conclusion, or select the most appropriate conclusion. There are many books that have been written on strategies for improving literacy and these should be referred to. The key element is that the literacy level should not be a barrier to accessing learning opportunities. The teacher should allow the student to access the highest levels of learning in a way that does not rely heavily on literacy skills.

The next section will provide some insight into using a range of teaching styles to suit all learners.

Multiple intelligences and learning styles

As science teachers looking at identifying gifted students, the temptation is to base our opinions on accepted experiences to date of what it means to be gifted. These may include our own exposure to peers, who are adults, and how they perform in the specialised field in which they, and we, work. For children, the measure of giftedness is made against other pupils within a large year group and across a range of subjects. It is thus important to understand how giftedness develops in children. Bloom and his colleagues (1985) identified three general phases in childhood development:

1. the playful phase

2. the precision phase

3. the personal style phase.

The playful phase involves enjoyment rather than aiming for achievement. The child may become involved in a field of interest and then pursue it because it is interesting to them.

The precision phase sees the child aiming for perfection and trying to master all the skills necessary to demonstrate excellence in their chosen field of interest.

The third phase comes about when a child is able to develop something original and completely new, using the talents they have mastered in the first two phases. The child is able to show a personal style in their area or areas of ability. It is unlikely that this third phase will come about until adolescence, making it hard to assess on entry to secondary school whether a child who has attained the precision phase in one or more fields will go on to the third phase. Furthermore, students at stage two may wish to remain at the precision phase, particularly if they find it satisfying. They may well not advance to stage three, becoming technically proficient but lacking any creativity or originality, as suggested by Gardner (2000). It is also worth noting that the progression from stage two to three may not be in a fashion which is recognisable or acceptable. Think about the student who is always asking about what would happen if you mixed the chemicals together in a different way, or added different combinations. Do we regard them as being original and creative in their thinking, or do we dismiss their actions as potentially dangerous?

Early identification of students with the potential to attain the personal style phase is thus difficult on entry to secondary school and this highlights the need to keep the gifted and talented cohort fluid, with students able to move in and out of the cohort. It also illustrates the need for subject-specific cohorts with waiting lists. Finally, it shows that attainment at GCSE does not automatically equate to attainment at A level as students may become comfortable at the precision phase.

In this book we are concerned with the gifted science student. That student may well be gifted in science only, or in a full range of subject areas. Gardner (1999) proposed eight possible areas of intelligence in which a student may display a high level of ability:

- bodily–kinaesthetic

- interpersonal

- intrapersonal

- linguistic

- logical–mathematical

- musical

- natural

- spatial.

While it is possible to find students who exhibit all the intelligences that Gardner proposed, it is more likely that the degree to which a gifted student exhibits each intelligence is uneven. Generic giftedness across all intelligences is rare.

Learning and teaching styles

It may be useful to use the teaching style analysis in Appendix 2.7 to audit the type of teaching that you do, and that which is going on in your department. Use the questionnaire in Appendix 2.6 to assess your own preferred learning style, and also let your students have a go. The letter (V, A or K) which scores the most indicates your preferred learning style. However, this does not mean that you

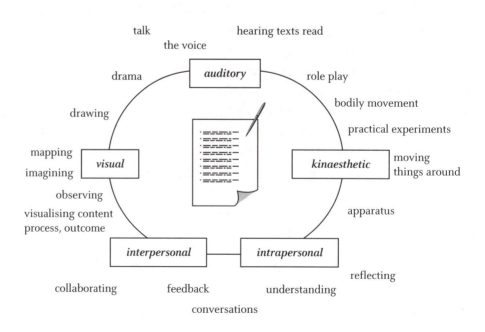

learn in only one way. In fact, it is important that students should try to develop a range of learning styles so that they can access different teaching styles deployed by different teachers.

The relationship between the learning styles is summarised in the diagram on page 48, taken from the Key Stage 3 National Strategy document *Learning Styles and Writing in Science* (DfES 2002).

Developing thinking

So far we have looked at how giftedness expresses itself. It is now essential that we look at how we can apply thinking skills to the science curriculum. The pressures of the curriculum means that much of the teaching and learning being delivered within our schools centres around knowledge and comprehension. Often the learning is short-term and lacks understanding. What is required is a deeper level of learning with more meaningful understanding, delivered through a range of experiences. To facilitate this it is necessary to have an understanding

Higher order thinking skills	Examples
Synthesis (create) Higher order thinking skills	● Create ● Compose ● Invent ● Hypothesize ● What would happen if . . . ● Design ● Be original ● Combine from several sources
Evaluation (judge) Higher order thinking skills	● Give opinion ● Judge ● Rate. i.e. best/worst ● Choose ● Recommend ● What to do differently
Analysis (relationships) Higher order thinking skills	● Categorise ● Compare/contrast ● Alike/different ● Cause/effect ● Relevant/irrelevant ● Find fallacies ● Fact/opinion
Application (use) Middle order thinking skill	● Use in other place or situation
Knowledge/comprehension Lower order thinking skills	● Tell ● Find ● Summarise in own words ● Locate ● Name

Bloom's building blocks

of Bloom's building blocks, a model of low, middle and higher order thinking skills.

It is important that we encourage children to operate in the higher order thinking skills area.

Case studies

Case study– Pupil with EAL

Noor is a 13-year-old Somali girl. When she arrived at school in Year 7 she spoke little English but her written English was good and very neat. She was very shy and quiet, rarely asking for help other than what was expected of her in the lesson. Noor was happy writing, copying text boxes and labelling text onto diagrams. She was placed in a lower set because she required additional support for EAL, and a small group allowed this. Staff focused their efforts on equipping Noor with the skills needed to access the content of science lessons – reading, writing and speaking English.

Noor quickly surpassed expectation for a low set. It was apparent from her test scores that she was able to reason out problems. At first it was not clear whether Noor had achieved well because of the additional support or because of a natural ability to reason scientifically. Noor was therefore challenged to a different kind of test – the ability to succeed in top set.

Noor was spoken to about the plan to move her group. She was delighted and confessed that she had found the work up to now very easy, although it had had the desired effect of improving her English skills.

The in-class support was withdrawn. Noor moved to set 1 in Year 8. The group contained a good mix of pupils who were working well together as a class and achieving easily the level 6 and 7 work that was being studied. Noor rose to the challenge and regularly ranked in the top 3 end-of-unit test scores. By the end of Year 8 she was achieving the top of level 6 convincingly. Noor enjoys science and aspires to a career in science.

Questions to consider:

- How could Noor have been assessed for innate ability in science?

- How would Noor have coped if she had gone straight in to set 1?

- Did Noor get access to the most suitable level of teaching and learning in Year 7? If not, how could this have been improved?

- How could her in-class support have been organised better?

- What are the cultural expectations placed on Noor?

- What would have been the impact on Noor if she had stayed in a low set?

- What would have been the impact on her peers if she had stayed in a low set?

- Would Noor have received suitable additional support and been successful in any school she attended?

- What procedures do you have in place for the identification and support of able pupils with EAL?

- What procedures are in place to raise the aspirations of pupils with EAL?

Case study – Very bright but uninterested and underachieving student

Mark is very difficult in class. He rarely brings any equipment. He arrives late. He does not acknowledge staff when he enters a room. Mark does not like to communicate with staff. He is not well liked by pupils because he disrupts lessons by clowning around. Written work is the bane of his life and so it is usually not completed. His lack of willingness to communicate with staff means that he is unpredictable during practical work and so is sometimes removed for safety reasons. His behaviour is similar across the curriculum.

Quite surprisingly, and I suppose annoyingly too, Mark regularly achieves in the top ten marks in set 1 for the end-of-unit tests, out of 30 pupils. He seems to have a natural ability to do well in tests. He does not do his homework, take part in revision lessons, take books home, answer practice questions in class or ask for any help. In fact, he doesn't even appear to ever be listening or taking in any information. So I think the natural question to ask is just how much better could Mark do if he were brought in to the lesson in a participative way? What could be done to encourage Mark?

This is a difficult question to answer unless you have met Mark, but I am sure that all teachers will have encountered someone similar. The first thing to do is identify the main primers which make Mark uncooperative. These are sitting in his place, writing and talking to staff. These are things that would seem non-negotiable by most staff, but just how important are they to the education of an able pupil such as Mark?

CHAPTER 4

Classroom provision

- Planning classroom provision
- Differentiation
- Teaching styles
- Extension and enrichment activities
- Skills needed by the more able and ways of developing them
- Applying Bloom's taxonomy of learning
- Using multiple intelligences

Planning classroom provision

Checklist for the science department

Some schools have already made significant progress in identifying and providing for the gifted science student. Other schools are still in the first stages of tackling the challenge. The most essential element is ensuring that all staff agree that this is a high-priority issue. Achievement at the higher levels at the end of each key stage indicates that many pupils do not fulfil their early promise and there is under-achievement, particularly among pupils from vulnerable and lower socio-economic groups.

> The real challenge is to set higher expectations for progress for all, because sustained progress will mean more pupil and parent engagement throughout the learning journey.
>
> (*Making good progress*, DfES 2007)

The aim is to have at least one leading teacher for G&T in each school. LAs will need to provide training so that all schools can have access to the support of a leading teacher for G&T education. Schools may identify existing coordinators or ASTs to take on the role, or decide to have two teachers working closely together, sharing the role.

There are two key aspects to the role of leading teachers for G&T education:

1. The development of whole-school self-evaluation and improvement planning for the provision and outcomes for G&T pupils.

2. The development of effective classroom practice for G&T pupils.

In planning the provision for able students within the department you may find the following checklist useful.

Departments must	• select a coordinator who can liaise with the school coordinator. • include provision in schemes of work. • ensure the scheme of work is challenging. • set challenging targets for able students. • identify students on class lists. • monitor use of differentiation. • monitor and evaluate learning and teaching strategies. • update and use departmental policy, which should support whole-school policy. • include provision for able students on DDP and departmental agenda.
Departments should	• consider a range of activities and resources for able students. • review budget spend on able students. • update training of staff and be aware of current thinking. • encourage greater use of higher order thinking skills.
Departments could	• evaluate targets and results achieved by able students. • offer enrichment activities that support learning in class. • organise science masterclasses. • offer early exam entry.

Checklist for the science department when planning provision for able students

In addition to this checklist, which focuses on the whole department, it is useful to note what individual teachers should consider when planning provision for able students.

The importance of undertaking an audit of current provision was discussed in Chapter 2. So, at this point, let us consider the following questions:

*   Do we differentiate by resources and materials?

*   Do we differentiate by tasks and subject content?

*   Is homework differentiated?

*   Do we differentiate by vocabulary used?

*   Do we differentiate by pace?

*   Do we set, or group, organised ability groups in class?

Teachers must	• ensure that students are identified on class lists and registers. • be aware of, use, and contribute to an inclusive scheme of work. • be familiar with whole-school and departmental policy. • use strategies to encourage able students. • differentiate for all able students.
Teachers should	• contribute ideas for extension and enrichment activities. • encourage independent learning. • use higher order thinking skills in lessons to develop pupils' learning.
Teachers could	• organise an extension or enrichment activity. • organise a masterclass or field trip.

Checklist for individual science teachers when planning provision for able students

All these methods of differentiation should be used in the context of supporting the whole-school strategies for greater impact and sustainability. It is also important to consider other aspects of planning:

- Do schemes of work have extension activities?

- Are resources and practical activities graded for higher ability?

- Does challenge exist in lessons?

- What challenges exist in extracurricular activities?

- Are staff supportive and capable of delivering the challenge?

The last point raises the issue of the importance of having a good professional development system within the school. The head of department is responsible for ensuring that all staff within that department are up to date with training in areas such as curriculum advances, variety of teaching methods, government initiatives, assessment for learning and so on. The most important resource within any gifted and talented programme is the teaching team. Teaching the gifted science student requires the teacher to be an expert in their subject knowledge and in their delivery of that knowledge using a wide variety of teaching strategies:

> Good teaching for the gifted and talented has the essential characteristics of good teaching for any pupil but is particularly dependent on the teachers' own specialist expertise and scholarship. In the best lessons seen, teachers' knowledge of the subject was very secure.
>
> *(Providing for Gifted and Talented Pupils: An Evaluation of Excellence in Cities and Other Grant-funded Programmes,*
> HMI 334 Ofsted December 2001)

Planning the staffing within the department therefore requires careful selection of those staff who will best meet the needs of the most able students. This is especially true for 14–19 provision, where subject specialists traditionally take over in science departments. Key Stage 3 is often taught by general science teachers owing to the lower level of knowledge required.

If staffing is an issue then the head of department should consider whether the matter could be resolved by:

- specific targeted professional development

- an alternative staffing structure

- using alternative subject expertise from outside agencies or institutions.

Case study – Gifted and talented peripatetic chemistry teacher

A large inner city comprehensive school required a chemistry teacher to assist with the teaching of the Year 11 dual science GCSE. There was only one chemistry teacher in the department of nine staff. The timetable would normally have been split so that the biology, chemistry and physics teacher had two lessons each. However, with timetabling constraints the chemistry teacher could not manage to teach GCSE chemistry to Year 10 and 11, both single and dual award. The biology and physics teachers split the lessons three each. The deputy head was able to timetable one biology and one physics lesson back to back to give a double chemistry lesson on one day.

The head of department contacted the Excellence in Cities coordinator in the LA who provided a gifted and talented peripatetic chemistry teacher to come in once each week for the double lesson, either side of lunch. The biology and physics teacher remained in the lesson with the peripatetic teacher, who was trained in teaching and supporting able pupils. As a result, not only did the pupils benefit from the expertise in subject knowledge and teaching strategies, but coaching of two members of staff took place on a weekly basis throughout the year.

Differentiation

What is the school already doing to address the issue of matching teaching and learning to the needs of the able student? There are four main areas that should be considered – differentiation, pace, resources and schemes of work. Let us look at each one in turn.

Differentiation

- within each unit of work
- by content
- by tasks given in the lesson
- by outcome
- by how you talk to students
- by expectation of the student
- by questions that you ask the students
- by materials, equipment and resources

- by grouping of students
- by seating arrangements within the classroom
- banding
- setting.

Pace

- Is the pace of each lesson challenging enough for an able pupil?
- Is the progression through the unit of work fast enough?
- Is the pace through the year maintaining the challenge?
- Is the pace through the Key Stages matching the ability of the student?

Resources

- Are they tiered or graded?
- Does the challenge exist to move on to the next level?
- Have you included challenging resources for low literacy students and EAL students?

Schemes of work

- Do you have clearly defined extension tasks within your schemes of work?
- Do you have differentiated homework?
- Is the scheme of work flexible enough to allow fast tracking?
- Can the scheme cope with compression for early SATs or GCSE entry?
- What's in it for the pupil?

Above all else, differentiation must be seen to be happening each day by the students. Once built into the schemes of work there should be monitoring and evaluation procedures in place so that the subject leader can be confident that the able students are receiving a challenging education. The benefit of differentiation is not just improved levels and grades, it is also maintaining interested students who do not switch off and become dissatisfied, underachieving science students. Encourage staff to use the must–should–could model of planning, as shown in the lesson plan pro forma in Appendix 4.1 and on the accompanying website.

Teaching styles

Once you have considered the content of differentiated lessons, you need to consider your own teaching styles. You may remember some of your own teachers who inspired you because they were enthusiastic, lively and passionate about their subject. Their enthusiasm was evident in all aspects of their teaching and rubbed off onto the students. Perhaps you remember walking out of a lesson talking about it and continuing to talk about it later, in the playground or with parents. Do you witness this in and out of your lessons?

It may be that you hear teachers in your department or in the staffroom saying things such as 'I can't teach because Phillip just keeps on asking questions. I wish he could just be quiet so I can get on with the lesson.' or 'I told Jenny that that work is at GCSE and so we will cover it then.' If this sounds familiar then you may be right in deducing that students are not being encouraged to attain their full potential.

Able children need challenge now and want to know answers now. They should not have to wait until Year 11. The students should be guided and pointed in the right direction to find out answers, through experiential learning.

That does not mean that you should find yourself doing large amounts of extra work. If the students are guided in the right direction with appropriate and challenging tasks, then that may well be sufficient to allow them to find the answers they need to a topic themselves.

Pupils should be encouraged towards independent learning. Dr Robert Fisher of Brunel University adapted Bloom's model to four levels of learning:

- Rote – basic thinking, repeating tasks

- Literal – applying a known procedure

- Analytical – analysis of results to make conclusions

- Conceptual – creating ideas from experience that can be applied elsewhere.

Fisher believes that any topic can be delivered at an analytical level and a conceptual level. This does not necessitate altering schemes of work. What needs altering is the method of delivery – the teaching style. The delivery of different topics can be evaluated by using a diagram of Fisher's four levels of learning. It is quite easy and straightforward filling in what is delivered by rote or literal learning. This type of delivery centres around the teacher, and so is more easily applied and controlled by the teacher. The challenge is in finding questions that will shift the delivery into the realms of analysis and concepts.

Incidentally, the analytical and conceptual levels of learning are not limited to the more able student. Students of all abilities can operate in higher order thinking. With this in mind it is worth noting that an effective programme to support more able students will have a positive impact on whole school improvement.

A model of Fisher's four levels of learning is shown below.

Analytical	Conceptual
Classifies, solves problems, reasons, questions, transforms, summarises.	Applies principles, understands key concepts, evaluates abstract ideas, forms new hypotheses.
Literal	Rote
Reads, re-tells, applies known procedures, communicates what is known.	Repeats, copies.

Fisher's four levels of learning

By analysing tasks in this way, teachers can challenge students to operate at higher order thinking levels and move beyond rote learning and literal comprehension. The example below focuses on a Year 7 lesson on the use of a Bunsen burner.

Analytical	Conceptual
How can you change the flame? Which is the hotter flame? How do you know? Why is it hotter?	Why has the Bunsen burner been designed this way? When would you use the different flames? What use is the orange flame?
Literal	Rote
Light the Bunsen burner and turn the air hole safely.	Follow the instructions and repeat.

Year 7 – Using a Bunsen burner (Fisher's model)

This example looks at the use of a force meter in Year 7.

Analytical	Conceptual
How can you measure a larger force? What is the relationship between force and length of spring? Is the scale appropriate?	Why has a spring been used? Design a meter with an elastic band? How accurate will it be? What are the limitations?
Literal	Rote
Use the force meter to measure the force on the objects.	Follow the instruction sheet to measure the force. Repeat for each object.

Year 7 – Using a force meter (Fisher's model)

This example shows the same model being used for the particles topic in Year 7.

Analytical	Conceptual
Explain how the model effectively represents each state? What things in your model should you change and what should you keep the same for each state?	Would the model be the same for mixtures, molecules or compounds? How could the model be improved? Instead of circles, what other model could you design to represent particles in the three states?
Literal	Rote
Use circles to show how the particles are arranged in a solid, a liquid and a gas. Put the appropriate label under each diagram.	Use the information on the worksheet to show the particles arranged in a solid. Repeat for a liquid and a gas.

Year 7 – Particles (Fisher's model)

Extension and enrichment activities

One of the first things that any teacher should do in looking to improve the extension and enrichment activities in the science department is to look at what is already taking place.

Case study

A new head of science joined a very successful and oversubscribed voluntary-aided secondary school. The school had a six form entry, with 30 pupils in each class. There was a very high percentage of students gaining five A–C grades. One of the first identified tasks was to improve the number of students gaining grade A/A*, which had remained at a level below similar schools for the previous three years. In response to this the head of department carried out an audit of provision of out-of-hours clubs and activities. She found that there were no science clubs. The audit also showed a pattern of enrichment at Key Stage 3 that was not matched at Key Stage 4. The audit results are shown below.

Year group	Activity	Outcome	Number taking part
8	GETSET/BETSET	Problem solving, teamwork, CREST award (bronze)	20 (maximum number allowed)
9	GETSET/BETSET	Problem solving, teamwork, CREST award (bronze, upgraded to silver in science club)	12 (maximum number allowed)
9	SATs revision	Level 7 SATs questions	75
9	Summer school	Forensic science	30
11	GCSE revision	Revise higher level work, analyse past papers	20
11	Summer school residential at local university.	Life at university – lectures and social activities	18 (maximum number allowed)
12	River study	Environmental study to support coursework	20
12	Nuffield bursary	Range of summer projects at University	4 (maximum number allowed)

Audit of extracurricular science activities

The students had willingly taken part in out-of-hours activities when they were in Years 8 and 9, but when these enrichment activities were not offered at Key Stage 4, the students became disengaged with the subject, also failing to support the GCSE revision classes. It was assumed that the students were too busy doing their GCSE studies to want to do extracurricular activities, or that it was not 'cool' to be seen in science after school. After speaking to a number of students, a questionnaire was devised and given to pupils in lessons to complete. Over 57% said that they would want a science club for GCSE students. Of those students who wanted a science club, 71% wanted it to help reinforce their studies, 18% wanted it to find out more about what they were learning in class and 11% wanted it just for fun after school.

> Ironically, the results may have shown that by not providing enrichment activities at Key Stage 4 the students had formed the opinion that the science department did not care about them as individuals, but only as statistics. The enrichment activities at Key Stage 3 had been very popular and enjoyable but had ceased at Key Stage 4 in favour of exam preparation only at the end of the course. This was not well attended.
>
> The department initiated a GCSE science club which met at the end of each half term to go over key learning objectives for the higher tier paper for the previous term.

Being informed about what activities are happening in your department is essential for good leadership. It is necessary for financial planning, staffing provision, development of resources and staff through professional training programmes, and in communicating to parents that the department values the contribution made by their children. Therefore it is advisable to plan the activities so that a timetable for the year can be drawn up. Activities that take place each year can be timetabled even if the exact date is not known. Share this information with students, parents and your school leadership group so that it can inform planning.

Skills needed by the more able and ways of developing them

Developing thinking skills

Thinking usually involves remembering information that we have previously learned and stored in our brains – our memory. This is simply an accumulation of knowledge and is often unconnected in our memory. It is a product of our exposure to the education system, one that emphasises the input of facts.

In our world today we need to be good at thinking in various ways – being critical, being creative, making connections in our memory in different ways. The fewer connections that we make in our memory, the less able we are at thinking. Think about the following bears: polar, brown, panda, grizzly, black. You will probably be able to think about them using all the qualities you have stored in your brain about 'bears'. However, what about the connection between the following: black bear, mountain lion, scorpion, rattlesnake, gila monster? You may know that the connection is the habitat, the Sonoran desert of south-western USA. The examples could start to get a little more obscure, but I hope we can develop the connections as we go through the chapter.

When analysing and learning new things your brain uses criteria to file the information away. We look for connections with previous files, e.g. mammals, colours, adjectives, symbols and so on. Some of our files already have a number of examples in them, depending on our previous learning and experiences. We may have even made connections between some of the files, e.g. mammals of a particular colour. To improve our thinking we must be good at noticing things about what it is we are learning, and asking ourselves questions about them. Mammals have similar features, but what questions would I ask myself if I saw an unfamiliar animal to classify? The more questions you can ask yourself, the better you will become at thinking.

Observing properties

When we look at objects we take a lot for granted. Many of the objects we use every day have been designed that way for a purpose. Do we know why? It is useful to look for properties and then ask yourself the reason for them. The following table was taken from a Year 7 lesson on developing observational skills in the forces unit.

Year 7 – Observing properties		
Object	Properties	Reason for property
Coin	thin round metal	lightweight handle easily Durable
Aeroplane tyre	rubber round tread	bends, flexible can roll smoothly grip road, friction
Sail		
Rope		
Cricket ball		

Observing similarities and differences

Have you ever thought about how things are similar and different at the same time? Often we are not taught how they are similar or different, they just end up in a file in our brain. A bird and a ball would not always go in the same file. But if we have stored up enough information about them, you will find some connections between them, as well as differences. They are both lightweight, aerodynamic, travel through the air, and yet one can maintain its flight, reproduce and feed, while the other can not.

The following example was taken from the Year 7 unit on the environment and feeding relationships. It was designed to be not out of context, so as to give the students confidence. If the example had referred to elements then the students might not have made the connection. Remember, we are developing thinking skills. We need to promote a culture of achievement in Year 7 so that they keep up the interest in developing their thinking skills further.

The examples given can act as a catalyst for further examples. It is common for students to develop their own questions using different habitats, animals and plants. Encourage this and allow them to test each other.

Year 7 – Observing similarities and differences		
Thing	Similarities	Differences
Banana and lemon	• yellow fruit • grow on trees • have skin	• shape • lemon is citrus • seeds
Pond and river	• .... • .... •	• .... • .... • ....
Dragonfly and pond snail	• .... • .... •	• .... • .... • ....
Reed and water-lily	• .... • .... •	• .... • .... • ....

Categorising

The ability to categorise is a necessary skill for linking things together in your memory. You need to find a common property or a connection that links all the examples together. Similarly, in finding out which is not a member of the category, you need to find the link that is not appropriate. In the example below, taken from the Year 7 unit on forces, the students had to identify which was the odd one out and give a reason for the similarities and for the difference.

Year 7 – Categorising		
Objects/concepts	Reason three are the same	Reason one is different
Echo, music, thunder, lightning	types of sound	type of light
Photosynthesis, shadow, respiration, photocell	needs light	releases energy
Friction, Newton, gravity, upthrust	types of force	unit of force
Lever, balanced, pivot, pulley	parts of a machine	describes the force

This exercise tests the ability to identify links and also the ability to express the reasons clearly. It is not enough simply to identify the odd one out. The student has to be able to express the thought processes taking place, thus revealing the files being used.

Comparing two things

When students are developing their skills at making links they may find it useful to practise the link-making process by doing a comparison exercise. In this exercise the student has to think about how two things are different and how they are the same. In his book *Teaching Our Children to Think*, Langrehr (2001) suggests using the acronym SCUMPS. Students should be encouraged to think about the size, colour, use, material, parts and shape of the two things they are comparing. The following example was taken from a Year 7 unit called simple chemical reactions. The students have to fill in the links that apply to each of two items individually, and also the link that applies to both items together.

Year 7 – Comparing		
Only . . .	Both . . .	Only . . .
iron is: • magnetic • solid • easily oxidised	are: • metals • conduct electricity • are shiny	mercury is: • a liquid • poisonous • very dense
oxygen is: • • •	are: • • •	chlorine is: • • •
sodium is: • • •	are: • • •	copper is: • • •

These last four sections have focused on observing properties, observing similarities and differences, categorising and comparing. They are good exercises for Key Stage 3 students to engage in to develop their thinking, linking and questioning. Remember that the more links we create, the better we become at thinking. However, in order to develop into the realms of analytical and conceptual thinking, we need to focus on a range of activities that develops these skills.

Developing analytical thinking

Analytical thinking is more than just looking for links between things. It involves making links, finding all the parts that make up the links and understanding how they are related. Once all these have been established you can use the information to solve problems and complete tasks.

A good exercise for identifying the small parts that make up a file is the relationship exercise.

Example – Relationship exercise

Moon is to earth as electron is to . . .
Positive is to negative as north is to . . .
Sun is to star as earth is to . . .
Nerve is to message as artery is to . . .
Friction is to force as heat is to . . .
Hydrogen is to element as water is to . . .
Oxygen is to gas as carbon is to . . .
Valve is to heart as iris is to . . .
H^+ is to acid as OH^- is to . . .

This exercise can be prepared in advance of a lesson and used as a starter or plenary. On the other hand, once the principles have been taught, the students enjoy and benefit more from writing their own relationships.

Visually representing information

Good thinkers are good at representing concepts in their minds using pictures. They can simplify, summarise and clarify large amounts of information using mind pictures. To develop this skill, students should practise writing down the visual representation so that they can see it, then commit this to memory. With time and practice the students should get better at representing large amounts of information as diagrammatic, picture or tabular data rather than verbose information.

The following example is taken from a Year 7 unit on classification of animals and plants. The students had to read a passage and decide how to group the animals depicted.

Example – Visual representation

On Mrs Reilly's farm the children found an array of animals. Some were earning their keep while others were enjoying the freedom to live without fear of predation or hunger. On the pond outside the pig enclosure, Susan saw mallard ducks, scooping water with their wide flat beaks as they filtered small invertebrates for their lunch. One mallard was settled on the side of the pond, above a mound of dead grass that secured three pale blue eggs. As she warmed the eggs, her head darted back and forth across the feathers on her back and wings, eliminating unwanted parasites.

The smell from the pig pen became unbearable. Seeing the pigs wallow in mud, even whilst suckling their newly born piglets, made Susan shiver with disgust. She preferred to look past the pond, where her favourite mare galloped around with her foal, demonstrating how to show off to best effect.

She stared dreamily, but was startled by a splash. At the near edge of the pond she noticed a frog in the reeds by a log. Near to him a mass of polka dot jelly beans glistened in the evening sun. His job done, he disappeared into the depths to replenish his energy reserves.

On top of the reeds, a dragonfly landed and curled its long, slender abdomen and deposited dozens of creamy white eggs. It too left, never to return to see their plight.

The students were asked to show the groups of animals as a diagram. Below you can see how one student depicted the groups.

Animals that look after their young	Animals that do not look after their young	Animals that can fly
horse	frog	duck
pig	dragonfly	dragonfly
duck		

Grouping animals in columns

The table shows that the student had thought about how to link the animals in more than one way. This allowed the student to make more connections. Below is another representation of the grouping by a different student.

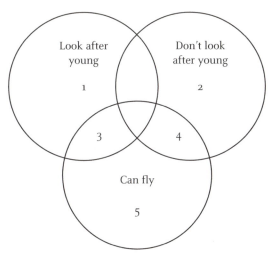

Grouping animals in overlapping circles

The student recommended that the animals should go into the following areas of the circles:

- duck – 3

- pig – 1

- horse – 1

- frog – 2

- dragonfly – 4.

Both students gave a good visual representation of the groupings. However, the second example showed more effectively the connections between some of the groups.

Critical thinking
Critical thinking involves asking questions so that you can make judgements. Langrehr (2001) suggested that we should use the acronym CAMPER to help us make judgements about what we read or learn:

- **Consequences** – What are the consequences of this belief?

- **Assumptions** – What are the assumptions being made?

- **Main issue** – What is the main issue being discussed?

- **Prejudice** – Is the information prejudiced in any way?

- Evidence/examples – What evidence is there to support this viewpoint? What are the examples of this?
- Reliable and relevant – How reliable and relevant is the information?

He also made the observation that good critical thinkers should be COOL! That is, they should try to:

- Clarify the issue
- be Objective about the issue by using data, facts and examples
- be Open-minded by considering all viewpoints
- be 'Loose' by modifying their viewpoint if they hear new facts.

So the recommendation is to be a COOL CAMPER when trying to think critically. The skill of critical thinking is one that runs through all of our intelligences (Gardner 1993), but whatever our particular strength we should aim to develop this skill.

Let us look at an example. A Year 8 class was studying unit 8C, microbes. They were asked to read a passage about microbes from the internet. The pupils were asked to decide whether the information in the text supported the article title.

The overwhelming majority of microbes in the world are not harmful.

Food processing researchers have established two kinds of microbes that are undesirable in food: spoilage microbes, which spoil the food but are not toxic to consume, and pathogenic microbes. Pathogens are harmful to consume, or they produce toxins that are harmful or fatal if consumed.

Researchers can identify which types of pathogenic and spoilage microbes are likely to be in a food based on its biological, chemical and physical properties. A processing method is then designed to ensure that these microbes will not grow or multiply in the food; this can be 'guaranteed' for only a certain period. For example, pasteurisation is a mild to moderate heat treatment designed to kill spoilage microbes. The consumer has 10 to 14 days to consume milk (if refrigerated) before spoilage microbes or yeasts sour the milk. In most other parts of the world, milk is subjected to heavy heat treatment (sterilisation) using aseptic processing. This milk lasts at least eight weeks and does not need to be refrigerated, even after being opened. Worldwide, most people drink milk warm or at room temperature.

What are microbes?

Microbes are tiny organisms – too tiny to see without a microscope – yet they are abundant on Earth. They live everywhere – in air, soil, rock, and water. Some of them live happily in searing heat, and others in freezing cold. Like humans, some microbes need oxygen to live, but others cannot exist with it. These microscopic organisms are in plants, animals, and in the human body.

Some microbes cause disease in humans, plants, and animals. Others are essential for a healthy life, and we could not exist without them. Indeed, the relationship between microbes and humans is very delicate and complex.

Most microbes belong to one of four major groups: bacteria, viruses, fungi, or protozoa. A familiar, often-used word for microbes that cause disease is 'germs'. Some people refer to disease-causing microbes as 'bugs'. 'I've got the flu bug,' for example, is a phrase you may hear during the wintertime to describe an influenza virus infection.

Since the 19th century, we have known microbes cause infectious diseases. Near the end of the 20th century, researchers began to learn that microbes also contribute to many chronic diseases and conditions. Mounting scientific evidence strongly links them to some forms of cancer, coronary artery disease, diabetes, multiple sclerosis, autism, and chronic lung diseases.

After reading the article the students had to write down whether they believed the information in the main body of the text did or did not support the title. They also had to provide evidence from the text to support their argument. The students were asked to apply the acronym CAMPER to help them make a judgement on the information presented. This technique is relatively quick and easy to apply in a classroom. It is advisable to search for a range of topics on the internet, scientific journals, newspapers and magazines. This gives the student the opportunity to experience a range of media and start to identify the difference between fact and opinion, which is essential in making judgements in science.

Consider the following example, which again refers to the Year 8 unit on microbes. The students are required to read the information. This would fit in after studying about types of microbes, conditions for growth, acquired immunity and the work of Edward Jenner. The article seeks to undermine the commonly held belief that Jenner discovered for himself the link between having mild forms of a disease and immunity, through his trials with milk maids and the boy James Phipps.

By way of an explanation of the article, Lady Montague travelled with her husband, the British ambassador, to the court of the Ottoman Empire in 1717. She wrote copious notes on her travels. In this extract she noted that the local practice of deliberately stimulating a mild form of smallpox through inoculation gave immunity. She had the procedure performed on both of her own children. By the end of the eighteenth century, Edward Jenner was able to cultivate a serum in cattle, which, when used in human vaccination, eventually led to the worldwide eradication of the illness.

A propos of distempers, I am going to tell you a thing that will make you wish yourself here. The small-pox, so fatal, and so general amongst us, is here entirely harmless, by the invention of engrafting, which is the term they give it. There is a set of old women, who make it their business to perform the operation, every autumn, in the month of September, when the great heat is abated. People send to one another to know if any of their family has a mind to have the small-pox; they make parties for this purpose, and when they are met (commonly fifteen or sixteen together) the old woman comes with a nut-shell full of the matter of the best sort of small-pox, and asks what vein you please to have opened. She immediately rips open that which you offer to her, with a large needle (which gives you no more pain than a common scratch) and puts into the vein as much matter as can lie upon the head of her needle, and after that, binds up the little wound with a hollow bit of shell, and in this manner opens four or five veins. The Grecians have commonly the superstition of opening one in the middle of the forehead, one in each arm, and one on the breast, to mark the sign of the Cross; but this has a very ill effect, all these wounds leaving little scars, and is not done by those that are not superstitious, who choose to have them in the legs, or that part of the arm that is concealed. The children or young patients play together all the rest of the day, and are in perfect health to the eighth. Then the fever begins to seize them, and they keep their beds two days, very seldom three. They have very rarely above twenty or thirty in their faces, which never mark, and in eight days time they are as well as before their illness. Where they are wounded, there remains running sores during the distemper, which I don't doubt is a great relief to it. Every year, thousands undergo this operation, and the French Ambassador says pleasantly, that they take the small-pox here by way of diversion, as they take the waters in other countries. There is no example of any one that has died in it, and you may believe I am well satisfied of the safety of this experiment, since I intend to try it on my dear little son. I am patriot enough to take the pains to bring this useful invention into fashion in England, and I should not fail to write to some of our doctors very particularly about it, if I knew any one of them that I thought had virtue enough to destroy such a considerable branch of their revenue, for the good of mankind. But that distemper is too beneficial to them, not to expose to all their resentment, the hardy weight that should undertake to put an end to it. Perhaps if I live to return, I may, however, have courage to war with them.

Source: *From Lady Mary Wortley Montagu*, Letters of the Right Honourable Lady Mary Wortley Montagu: Written During her Travels in Europe, Asia and Africa . . ., vol. 1 (Aix: Anthony Henricy, 1796), pp. 167–9; letter 36, to Mrs. S. C. from Adrianople, n.d.

Tasks for students:

1. Can you identify one sentence that shows that Lady Montagu is expressing her opinion?

2. What direct observations did Lady Montagu make?

3. Underline any information that is irrelevant to her conclusions?

4. Has Lady Montagu made any assumptions?

5. How reliable is her evidence?

6. Can you predict the consequence of her actions suggested in the final sentence?

7. Do you think Lady Montagu is prejudiced in any way? What suggests it?

Developing creative thinking

Creative thinking involves diversifying your thinking, trying to break away from patterns of conformity in your thinking. We spend a lot of time training students to conform:

- pencil and ruler for ray diagrams
- straight lines for circuit diagrams
- capital letter/lower case letter for chemical symbols
- arrows left to right in food chains.

When we want our students to be creative, we must stimulate them with some ideas about what it means to be creative. Langrehr (2001) suggested the acronym CREATE:

- **Combine** – Can I combine some things in a new way?
- **Reverse** – Can I reverse some parts or processes?
- **Eliminate** – Can I eliminate or remove some parts or processes?
- **Alternative** – Can I use alternative methods or materials?
- **Twist** – Can I twist things around a little?
- **Elaborate** – Can I elaborate or add something?

Case study

A group of Year 10 mixed ability students were studying the effect of skin hairs on temperature regulation. They had learned that the hairs stand up when the skin receptors detect a fall in temperature, so as to trap a layer of air which acts as an insulator next to the skin. They were asked to give a reason why, if hairs were there to keep us warm, they were so sparsely spread on most people. They were asked to devise a method of testing any theory they proposed. One student wrote the following plan for an experiment.

In Year 7 we investigated the properties of materials, using beakers and a range of materials. I think we should adapt that experiment. If we fill 3 beakers with hot water, they can represent our body heat. I will need to monitor the temperature of the water in those beakers each minute using a data logger connected to my computer. On top of the beaker, heat will escape by convection. To reduce this I will place a layer of material across the top to represent the skin hairs. I will use 3 materials of increasing density, but same thickness of material. I would expect the following to happen:

- In the beaker with the most dense material, the temperature will stay highest. This is actually a bad thing because our body needs to lose heat sometimes.

- In the beaker with the medium density material, the temperature will fall a little more.

- In the beaker with the least dense material, the temperature will fall the most, but not a lot more. Also, I think I will see steam coming through the fibres. This would be similar to sweat coming from our skin. I think having fewer hairs is good because it allows us to balance keeping warm with losing heat by evaporation of sweat. This is called homeostasis.

The student showed her ability to think about previous experiences, combine them in a new way, use an alternative method, twist things around a bit, reverse the thinking on the expected outcome, and elaborate on the prediction given – a good example of a creative thinker.

There is more information on thinking skills at the website dedicated to this topic: www.teachingthinking.net.

Applying Bloom's taxonomy of learning

Learning is a complex and multi-faceted process. Benjamin Bloom was an American professor of education who devised a taxonomy for different forms, or domains, of learning. He placed these domains of learning into three categories:

- **Cognitive learning** – shown by knowledge recall and the application of intellectual skills. This domain has been the subject of a huge amount of research and analysis.

- **Affective learning** – shown by the ability to respond with appropriate emotions, attitudes and values when interacting with people.

- **Psychomotor learning** – shown by the development of physical and motor skills.

Bloom proposed that each domain is organised in a series of different levels. He argued that the ability of a person to perform at one level depended on their ability to perform at the level previous to it.

Science teachers are primarily concerned with the cognitive domain in their daily teaching and learning. However, psychomotor learning is required in order to perform a range of practical activities in the science lab. Weakness in affective learning may not prevent students from excelling in the science curriculum but strengths in this area may enable the student to work more effectively in groups and with the teacher.

So, for now we will focus on the aspects of cognitive learning that can help us to improve the learning that takes place in our classroom. Cognitive learning is about picking up and using knowledge. In his work, Bloom identified six levels within the cognitive domain, with each level becoming increasingly more complex. These levels are shown below, with a few words that characterise the complexity of that level.

Level	Characteristic abilities
Knowledge	Name, label, list, state, repeat, show, recognise, order, redo
Comprehension	Describe, explain, discuss, select, identify, group, summarise
Application	Demonstrate, apply, use, illustrate, solve
Analysis	Compare, contrast, analyse, criticise, differentiate, test, examine
Synthesis	Design, propose, formulate, develop, create, plan
Evaluation	Assess, evaluate, rate, predict, reflect, select, improve.

Bloom's taxonomy (cognitive domain)

It is beneficial for us to look at our schemes of work and identify at what level of cognitive learning we are teaching our students. For our most able students the questions that we ask, the worksheets that we use and the homework that we set should reflect the level of synthesis and evaluation. If we only ask students to name, label, cut out and organise, then we are not challenging our most able learners to develop further.

As a quick exercise, take out a few worksheets that you anticipate using in the next week. Look for the words that reflect the knowledge and comprehension levels of learning. Now try to re-word those questions with ones that reflect analysis, synthesis and evaluation.

Look at the picture of a palisade cell inside a leaf.

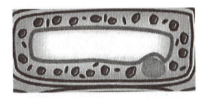

1. Explain why the cell is this shape.
2. Draw the diagram into your book.
3. Label the chloroplasts.
4. Write out the word equation for photosynthesis.

Worksheet – Looking at photosynthesis in plant cells

The questions above are not challenging and only require the student to 'do' rather than think. In the amended worksheet below, the student must understand the structure and role of chloroplasts, as well as recall, analyse, synthesise and evaluate prior knowledge in order to complete the tasks successfully.

Look at the picture of a palisade cell inside a leaf.

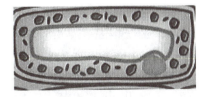

1. Compare the shape of a palisade cell with a spongy mesophyll cell.
2. Can you improve upon the design of a palisade cell?
3. Compare and contrast a chloroplast with a mitochondrion.
4. Predict the impact of increased light intensity on chloroplast number.

Worksheet – Looking at photosynthesis in plant cells

Using multiple intelligences

The theory of multiple intelligences was developed in 1983 by Howard Gardner, professor of education at Harvard University. It suggests that the traditional notion of intelligence, based on IQ testing, is far too limited. Instead, Gardner proposed eight different intelligences to account for a broader range of human potential in children and adults. These intelligences are:

- **Kinaesthetic** – You enjoy sports and are good at swimming, athletics, gymnastics and other sports, primarily due to good balance and coordination.

- **Logical** – You are good at mathematics and other number activities; you are also good at solving problems. Patterns in numbers are easy to see and you can identify trends and anomalies in data.

- **Intrapersonal** – You know about yourself and your strengths and weaknesses. You probably keep a diary. You can recognise changes in your mood or behaviour and are able to account for them.

- **Visual/spatial** – You are good at art and also good at other activities where you look at pictures, such as map reading, finding your way out of mazes and interpreting graphs. You have a good sense of direction and can visualise journeys to places. Orienteering may be a strength.

- **Linguistic** – You enjoy reading, writing and talking about things. You enjoy words for their sound, meaning, origin or rhythm. You like playing with words and twisting their meaning.

- **Interpersonal** – You like to mix with other people and you belong to clubs, teams and/or societies. You like team games and are good at sharing. You can relate to others easily and can understand their body language, behaviour, moods and emotions.

- **Musical** – You enjoy music and can recognise sounds, and timbre, or the quality of a tone. You understand how music can relate to concrete ideas such as seasons and abstract ideas such as emotions. When listening to music you can feel emotions and understand how changes in key, tempo or loudness cause this.

- **Naturalistic** – You like the world of plants and animals and enjoy learning about them. You understand the relationships between living things and what affects them.

According to Gardner, our schools and culture focus most of their attention on linguistic and logical–mathematical intelligence. We value articulate or logical people in our culture. However, Gardner suggested that we should also place equal attention on individuals who show gifts in the other intelligences: the artists, architects, musicians, naturalists, designers, dancers, therapists, entrepreneurs, and others who enrich the world in which we live. Unfortunately, some children who have these gifts do not receive reinforcement for them in school. Many of these students, in fact, end up simply underachieving, when their unique ways of thinking and learning are not addressed by a heavily linguistic or logical–mathematical classroom.

The theory of multiple intelligences proposes a major transformation in the way our schools are run. It suggests that teachers should be trained to present their lessons in a wide variety of ways using music, cooperative learning, art activities, role play, multimedia, field trips, inner reflection, and much more. The good news is that the theory of multiple intelligences has had an impact on many educators, and schools are currently using its philosophy to redesign the way they educate children. The bad new is that there are still schools out there that teach in the same old way, through dry lessons and unchallenging worksheets with little variety and thick, wordy textbooks. The challenge is to get this information out to many more teachers, school administrators and others who work with children, so that each child has the opportunity to learn in ways more in keeping with the ways their unique minds work and learn.

The theory of multiple intelligences also has strong implications for adult learning and development. Many adults find themselves in jobs that do not make optimal use of their most highly developed intelligences (for example, the highly bodily–kinaesthetic individual who is stuck in a linguistic or logical office job when he or she would be much happier in a job where they could move around, such as a sports leader, a park ranger or a physiotherapist). The multiple intelligences theory gives adults a whole new way to look at their lives, examining potentials that they left behind in their childhood (such as a love for art or drama) but now have the opportunity to develop through courses, hobbies or other programmes of self-development. It is important as a teacher of science that you know your own strengths, so that you use them to your advantage in your teaching, but also that you are aware that not all students will appreciate your particular intelligence strengths. You should consider teaching in ways that allow the whole spectrum of intelligences to benefit.

How to teach or learn anything in eight different ways

One of the most remarkable features of the theory of multiple intelligences is how it provides eight different potential pathways to learning. If a teacher is having difficulty reaching a student in the more traditional linguistic or logical ways of instruction, the theory suggests several other ways in which the material might be presented to facilitate effective learning. Whatever you are teaching or learning, see how you might connect it with:

- words (linguistic intelligence)

- numbers or logic (logical–mathematical intelligence)

- pictures (spatial intelligence)

- music (musical intelligence)

- self-reflection and evaluation (intrapersonal intelligence)

- a physical experience (bodily–kinaesthetic intelligence)

- a social experience (interpersonal intelligence)

- an experience in the natural world (naturalist intelligence).

For example, if you are teaching or learning about the law of conservation of matter in chemistry, you might read about it (linguistic), study mathematical formulas that express it (logical–mathematical), examine a graphic chart that illustrates the principle (spatial), observe the law in the natural world (naturalist) or in the human world of commerce (interpersonal); examine the law in terms of your own body, e.g. balancing the equation for respiration in your body cells (bodily–kinaesthetic and intrapersonal), and/or write a song or find an existing song (musical) that demonstrates the law.

You do not have to teach or learn something in all eight ways: rather just consider what the possibilities are, and then decide which particular pathways interest you the most, or seem to be the most effective teaching or learning tools. The theory of multiple intelligences is so intriguing because it expands our horizon of available teaching/learning tools beyond the conventional linguistic and logical methods used in most schools (such as lectures, textbooks, writing assignments, formulas, etc.). To get started, put the topic of whatever you are interested in teaching or learning about in the centre of a blank sheet of paper, and draw eight straight lines or 'spokes' radiating out from this topic. Label each line with a different intelligence. Then start brainstorming ideas for teaching or learning that topic and write down ideas next to each intelligence. This is a spatial–linguistic approach of brainstorming; you might want to do this in other ways as well, using a tape recorder, having a group brainstorming session, etc.

Implementing Gardner's theory in the classroom

Having a clear understanding of the theory of multiple intelligences is only a starting point. Teachers must understand how this can assist them in supporting their students in the classroom. In fact, Gardner himself had his own view on how the theory should be implemented in the classroom. He said: 'It's very important that a teacher take individual differences among kids very seriously ... The bottom line is a deep interest in children and how their minds are different from one another, and in helping them use their minds well.'

Once this understanding of the different ways that children learn is embedded, teachers can start to plan to implement strategies that support their learning strengths. This is often achieved through adaptations of the curriculum. In her article 'Variations on a theme – how teachers interpret MI theory', Linda Campbell (1997) described five approaches to curriculum change:

- **Lesson design.** In order to stimulate all students, it is important to know your students' intelligence strengths. The teaching style of the lesson should reflect this, as well as giving students the opportunity to develop in other intelligence areas, for variety. It may be beneficial to use student voice and ask the students which styles of learning they find most stimulating for each unit of work they study.

- **Interdisciplinary units.** Secondary schools often include cross-curricular units, e.g. English and History to teach about the Great War, or Science and Physical Education to teach about respiration.

- **Student projects.** When given the opportunity to manage their own projects, students often use their own intelligence strengths. This can lead to a greater level of detail and understanding, allowing deeper learning to take place.

- **Assessments.** Instead of assessing whether a student has met the criteria for passing a test, it may be better to assess what the student has actually learned. Again, using student voice and in negotiation with the students, assessments can be devised by the students themselves that allow them to use their own intelligence strengths whilst simultaneously meeting the assessment criteria for each unit of work. This depends on how effective the teacher is in sharing the learning objectives with each student.

- **Apprenticeships.** These are already in place in many secondary schools. They allow students to gradually build up a skill until they are proficient.

Building up an intelligence profile on each class can therefore be a very useful tool in enabling all your students to succeed. By sharing this with all teachers and parents we can allow students to explore and learn in many ways, taking control and ownership of their learning. By applying their learning to real life experiences teachers and parents can help students have a greater insight into their own understanding and prepare them for a lifetime of learning.

CHAPTER 5

Support for learning

- Support for more able pupils with special needs
- Learning mentors
- Links with parents

Support for more able pupils with special needs

Pupils with physical, sensory, emotional or other special educational needs (SEN) may also be very able in terms of understanding science. When assessing such pupils, it is important to give opportunities for such strengths to be shown and thus recognised and developed further. This may require considerable curriculum modification and the use of specialist equipment, e.g. communication aids, adapted technology, Braille, tape recorder. Specific disorders may mask particular strengths, gifts and talents, for example:

- **Autism spectrum** – pupils may lack social and communication skills. Their 'odd' behaviour may overshadow scientific skill.

- **Specific learning difficulties/dyslexia** – pupils' talents and gifts may be masked by poor numeracy and/or literacy skills. Such pupils are likely to experience low self-esteem and considerable frustration. Recognition of particular strengths is very important in raising self-esteem and peer credibility.

- **Physical difficulties**, e.g. cerebral palsy and associated difficulties, may be so encompassing that an agile mind can sometimes be under-challenged. Careful learning assessment over time is particularly important for pupils with physical difficulties.

- **Sensory impairments** such as hearing loss or vision impairment do not themselves limit intellectual capacity. Pupils with such difficulties need to be given ample opportunity to show the gifts they possess.

- **Emotional and behavioural difficulties** often mask a pupil's true potential. This is particularly the case with pupils who have not been identified as gifted or talented and so may feel frustrated and experience low self-esteem.

Some of these learning barriers will be discussed through this chapter, which will focus on the characteristics of the learning difficulty and on solutions through classroom provision and use of additional adults such as teaching assistants.

Autism spectrum

People with autism and Asperger syndrome generally experience three areas of difficulty:

- social interaction

- social communication

- rigidity of thought.

Autism is a lifelong developmental disability that affects the way a person relates and communicates with people around them. Whether they are young children or adults, they have difficulty in relating in any meaningful way to their family and the people they meet. Their associated learning difficulties may be varied but they all share a common difficulty in making sense of the world in which they live. Repetitive behaviour patterns and resistance to change in their routine are characteristic. Children with Asperger syndrome differ in that they often want to be sociable and enjoy human contact. They may speak fluently but often will not take much notice of the person listening, coming across as overprecise and quite literal. They may also be obsessive about a hobby such as collecting things or memorising facts.

Asperger syndrome is one of a range of autism-like disorders which often manifest in 'eccentric' behaviour rather than obvious disability. It was first identified as a separate condition in 1944 by a German doctor, Hans Asperger, who spotted similar, odd behaviours in more than one of his patients. Often someone with Asperger may be obsessed with complex topics such as music, history or the weather, and have above-average verbal skills. But the voice may appear flat and emotionless, with speech being stilted or repetitive, and conversations tend to revolve around self rather than others. Many have dyslexia or writing problems, and can appear to lack common sense. While people with Asperger syndrome are frequently socially inept, many have above-average intelligence and they may excel in fields such as ICT and science.

Strategies for the teacher

The following ideas are useful for planning your lessons:

- Get the pupils' attention before addressing the class or they may not know you are talking to them.

- Use lots of visual support materials. Back up oral instructions with writing or drawings.

- Vary your questioning style.

- Sitting may be a problem. If they have dyspraxic tendencies they may prefer to stand. Point out pupils who are already sitting to help clarify your instructions.

- Avoid eye contact or direct attention.

- Take an interest in what they know about and let them share it with the class.

- Let them make things, such as models, games and cartoons.

- Encourage the use of non-competitive games, such as taking turns or loop cards.

- Keep to a classroom routine. Print up a checklist.

Science lesson checklist

Hang my coat up as soon as I enter class.

Get my pen, pencil and ruler out and put my bag away.

Write the title and date neatly from the board.

I put up my hand and wait when I want to ask a question.

Stay in my seat and listen to the teacher for instructions.

More information is available on the National Autistic Society's website at www.nas.org.uk.

Strategies for science teaching assistants

Having a teaching assistant (TA) can really help a student with Asperger syndrome to understand what to do and how to go about doing it. The TA should decide on a suitable place for the student to sit – somewhere comfortable and away from doors to avoid distraction. Be precise when giving instructions:

Now, Jane, I would like you to take out your green science exercise book and open it at the last page on which you did your work. Can you use your blue pen to copy the title and date from the board? That's great, Jane, now please look at Mrs Woods and listen to what instructions she is giving you. You can see the girls over there are looking and listening.

Encourage your TA to identify the non-verbal signals that are occurring in the classroom. These may include standing and waiting for quiet or the teacher writing notes on the board. Help the student to understand what to do by pointing out what others are doing:

> Look, Mary is wearing her safety glasses over her eyes. She has the Bunsen burner on a yellow safety flame.

Do not put pressure on the student. If the routine changes, such as when a teacher is absent, allow the student to regain their confidence in a quiet area or other room. The TA can assist the teacher by keeping records of the child's progress, which can inform the planning and differentiation process.

Case study – Malcolm, Year 7 (Asperger syndrome)

In spite of careful liaison between the primary school and the head of Year 7, teachers were still taken by surprise when they met Malcolm. They had not appreciated that he would have to be taught many things that other children pick up by observation. For instance, he did not understand about queuing for his lunch and simply crawled between everyone's legs to get to the food.

His speech is robotic and it can be disconcerting when he does not give the expected answer but simply says whatever is in his head at the time. He does not understand tact and might say 'That dress is old,' without appreciating that this could give offence. Sometimes he becomes obsessed by a door or window and wants it opened to a particular angle. This same obsession is apparent in his written work where he can become anxious if teachers try to persuade him to set it out in a different way.

He is a very able mathematician and should reach university level in three or four years. However, he cannot cope with group work or group investigations and will become quite agitated if put into such a situation. Malcolm is also an outstanding chess player and was representing the school within a few weeks of arriving. In all other academic subjects he copes quite well in the top set although his very literal understanding of some concepts can create problems.

Sport is a mystery to him. He does not understand the rules and is, in any case, lumbering and ungainly. It is during these lessons that his peers are most likely to be unkind, although, on the whole, they are quite protective towards him.

Strategies

- Support for Malcolm should be coordinated across the school, with one person responsible for monitoring him on a regular basis and dealing with any recurrent problems. The science teacher should approach this colleague for specific advice.

- Teach any social skills he lacks in a very simple and direct way. For example, 'When someone says "I'll help you" you say, "Thank you".'

- Where Malcolm finds group work distressing, he could work as one of a pair in which he has a specific task to accomplish that does not demand long periods of interaction.

- Acknowledge Malcolm's successes and encourage other pupils to be proud of his achievements in science.

Dyslexia

The definition of dyslexia used by the Dyslexia Institute is as follows:

> Dyslexia causes difficulties in learning to read, write and spell. Short-term memory, maths, concentration, personal organisation and sequencing may also be affected. It arises from a weakness in the processing of language-based information.

Problems may include difficulty in remembering a list of instructions; problems with getting thoughts together and sequencing for writing tasks such as planning investigations; poor organisation; good orally but can not put ideas down in words; poor spelling; forgets scientific symbols and their meanings. However, pupils with dyslexia are often very creative and imaginative.

Strategies for teachers

The following ideas are useful for planning your lessons:

- Leave notes on board as long as possible, or use flip charts.

- Use several different coloured board markers.

- Give a summary handout at the end.

- Allow word processing, especially for coursework.

- Mark positively.

- Provide keyword lists.

- Give out homework on a sheet with prompts and keywords to help them get started.

Case study – Michael, Year 9 (dyslexic)

Michael obtained a place at a boys' grammar school but has struggled ever since. He has an extensive vocabulary and always volunteers for drama productions and reporting back when working in a group in science. He does this very well. As well as science, he enjoys music, art and D&T and brings a keen imagination and wit to all these subjects. Michael prefers the company of teachers and older pupils, with whom he likes to debate topical issues. His peers, on the other hand, regard him as a' bit of a wimp' as he does not enjoy sport and frequently corrects their behaviour.

   After a very slow start in early childhood, Michael can now read fluently but his other problems associated with dyslexia remain. His spelling and handwriting are very poor. He finds it almost impossible to obtain information from large swathes of text. Even when the main ideas are summarised for him in bullet points, he still has difficulty revising for examinations or tests or picking out and organising the main ideas for an essay. The layout of his work is often chaotic and he finds it difficult to organise things in a way that is logical to other people. This can disguise his often very thorough understanding. His family is very supportive and give him a lot of help with homework, so much so that teachers are sometimes misled into believing that he is coping well, until his difficulties are highlighted by his very poor performance in written exams.

Because he is so articulate, Michael is able to explain his frustrations to his teachers who are, on the whole, sympathetic. However, they are not very helpful in providing him with useful strategies.

Strategies

- Liaise with the SEN team so that your approach with Michael fits in with their overall support programme for him.

- Teach Michael to mind map so that he can use this skill to record information and revise if he finds this helpful.

- Encourage Michael to remember facts by making audio recordings or setting them to music.

- Make sure that homework tasks are suitable for his level of ability but are modified to allow him to succeed. For example, give him a template of notes with key words missing rather than asking him to make his own notes.

- Encourage him to word process some homework and insist on careful use of a spellchecker.

Dyspraxia

The definition of dyspraxia used by the Dyspraxia Foundation is as follows:

Dyspraxia is an impairment or immaturity of the organisation of movement. It is an immaturity in the way the brain processes information, which results in messages not being properly or fully transmitted. Dyspraxia affects the planning of what to do. In many individuals there may be associated problems with language, perception and thought.

Dyspraxia may affect as many as one in ten of the population. The condition is also sometimes referred to as developmental dyspraxia or developmental coordination disorder. Males are four times more likely to be affected than females. Therefore, it is possible that there will be a child with dyspraxia in one of the classes you teach.

Strategies for teachers
The following ideas are useful for planning your lessons:

- Give the pupil a classroom responsibility such as handing out books or giving out equipment.

- Involve the pupil in group work through careful selection of partners for practical investigation work.

- Allow extra time for setting up equipment and putting it away.

- Use short sequences of instructions, and reinforce them often.

- Use diagrams and charts to facilitate understanding. Flow charts and sequenced diagrams of equipment being set up are suitable.

- Use wide-lined paper to allow for oversized writing.

- Refer frequently to classroom rules but also use praise often.

Strategies for science teaching assistants

The science TA can offer support by preparing materials in advance for the student with dyspraxia. Use symbols or pictures to help understanding and establish key points. For example, use diagrams of equipment that they can arrange in sequence prior to starting a practical investigation. It is sometimes necessary to act as a scribe, allowing the student to carry on with a learning activity whilst the TA records evidence or results. This can be made even more manageable by using a tape recorder that can be transcribed later if the TA is unavailable or busy supporting a range of pupils in the class. Provide access to a computer to encourage the production of neat, well-presented work, which can then be followed up with plenty of praise.

Support the work of the teacher by going over keywords and their meanings and uses. Ensure that the student has all the necessary resources to complete homework tasks at home. A note to parents to explain further or to clarify learning objectives can be placed in the student planner.

ADHD

Case study – Trevor, Year 8 (ADHD)

Trevor had the highest aggregated CAT score when he entered his comprehensive school but was described by his primary teachers as having a 'self-destruct button'. He is a bundle of contradictions. On good days he is capable of being charming and polite. Sometimes he becomes so engrossed in an activity that it is hard to draw him away from it. He loves books, especially those with detailed maps and diagrams in, and likes to share what he has found out with teachers and other adults. He is a natural actor and sings and looks like an angel.

Yet Trevor is equally capable of destroying a lesson with his extremely disruptive and increasingly dangerous behaviour. He will erupt from his stool and turn on a machine just as someone puts their hands near it. His science teachers have had to give up all practical lessons and lock the preparation room when he is around because he uses his intelligence and wide reading to destructive effect. He has an intense dislike of writing and rarely does class work or submits homework.

For a small band of troublesome peers, he is a hero. Most other pupils laugh at his antics but find him very disturbing. They are rarely brave enough to offer criticism.

His mother will not acknowledge that there is a problem and refuses to consider medication or psychiatric help.

Strategies

- Investigate the possibility that he is dyslexic if this has not already been done.

- Agree a school-wide policy of support, and even containment.

- Prioritise what behaviour or work is to be achieved and put in place a reward system. It might be best to make no demands as far as written work is concerned until the behaviour has been dealt with.

- Invite his mother to sit in on some lessons where the problems are most severe and keep trying to work with her.

Learning mentors

Learning mentors are one of the three main strands of the Excellence in Cities (EiC) initiative. They work with teaching and pastoral staff to identify, assess and work with pupils who need help to overcome barriers to learning. Amongst others, these barriers can include:

- behavioural problems

- bereavement

- difficulties at home

- problems transferring from primary to secondary school

- poor study or organisational skills.

Pupils suffering multiple disadvantages are a particular priority for support. The key focus of the work is supporting children and raising standards of achievement.

> Learning mentors are making a significant effect on the attendance, behaviour, self-esteem and progress of the pupils they support . . . the most successful and highly valued strand of the EiC programme . . . In 95% of the survey schools, inspectors judged that the mentoring programme made a positive contribution to the mainstream provision of the school as a whole, and had a beneficial effect on the behaviour of individual pupils and on their ability to learn and make progress.
>
> (Excellence in Cities and Education Action Zones: management and impact. HMI 1399, Ofsted 2003: 46)

Learning mentors free teachers to teach, and they can transform young people's attitudes towards school, their ability to cope with the challenges that they face, and ultimately their ability to achieve their true potential.

The work of a learning mentor typically takes the form of regular one-to-one sessions with children identified as requiring help, during which they and the child will agree targets for areas of concern (e.g. attendance, behaviour and attainment), and talk through any concerns the child might have regarding learning.

Learning mentors will typically form a relationship with the child, with the school staff and with the parents or carers in order to improve the child's engagement with learning.

More information on learning mentor provision for schools is available at www.standards.dfes.gov.uk/learningmentors/.

Case study, from a learning mentor

Louise was referred to me by her head of year. Her behaviour in and out of school had deteriorated and was having a knock-on effect on staff, pupils and her schoolwork, to the extent of her attacking another pupil for no apparent reason. She also started playing truant from school.

In my initial meeting with Louise, she said that she was very sorry for what she had done to the girl, and could not understand why her behaviour had deteriorated so much. She hated being dubbed a bully, and the only explanation she could give for her behaviour was her hormones.

Louise said that she 'messed about' in science, because she was bored and did not understand what the teacher wanted her to do in the lesson, and she could not be bothered to ask the teacher to explain.

I worked with Louise on a one-to-one basis in her science class as a support and as a mentor on a one-to-one basis in the office. Over a period of two months, she showed great improvement in both her attitude to work and to other pupils.

I got Louise involved in extracurricular lessons, such as dance, rock challenge and gospel choir. I finished mentoring her in May, but I still go to her science classes to keep her focused, because while she used to mess around a lot, she was actually able to articulate her scientific understanding exceptionally well to me. She did not want to show it for fear of negative comments from her peers.

When I first telephoned Louise's parents, they were relieved that someone was mentoring her, because her behaviour and attitude had changed suddenly. Her parents are happy that the mentoring sessions have worked and they have seen a great improvement, but want me to keep an eye on her.

Mentors are useful when meetings with gifted science students do not take place as frequently as you would like. Often the students only meet with the school coordinator once or twice each year. This is not enough, as students want to discuss issues, ask for support, relay positive experiences and have a chance to feel valued. The case study below is from a school experiencing difficulties meeting with students. The school used a mix of staff mentors and the school special educational needs coordinator (SENCO) for a mentoring project. The SENCO provided packs for the mentors containing the following information:

- an IEP for each student

- SAT levels and raw scores

- CAT scores

- recent test/exam results

- copies of communications with parents since last review

- any other relevant documents.

In this way, mentors were supplied with information enabling them to build up a profile of each student, their strengths and any current weaknesses or areas for support .

A simple form was provided to be completed by the mentor identifying current progress, student views/issues, targets and actions.

Case study – Using the SENCO and mentors

Eight teachers in a mentoring team were allocated a group of ten students across the age range. A gender balance was maintained as far as possible. Some effort was made to match individual students' strengths with the mentors' specialisms. The mentors kept the same group of mentees each year, adding new Year 7 students as the Year 11 students moved on. A key aspect of the session was target-setting, based on class activities.

A mentor would typically see two students per week during a 50 minute period. All staff in the team had 'mentoring time' on their timetable at the same time each week. The regular review sessions helped to identify and respond to individual needs of students, who valued the opportunity to talk about their needs and support requests.

Although there was general confidentiality, some issues and their resolution might not have come to light without the mentoring opportunities. Before the project started there was no support for the G&T cohort, or discussion of progress, interests and needs. A two-way dialogue was established on a regular basis, enabling far greater responsiveness to the needs of the cohort and greater awareness of the impact of the G&T programme.

Success factors included:

- the creation of a team of staff with the necessary qualities and experience

- safeguarded time which was always available for the mentoring project

- suitable places for the mentoring to take place, which created a safe and confidential environment

- support from the senior management of the school.

Links with parents

Parents are a child's primary educator. It is important to remember that the whole purpose of a school is to help a family to educate a child. With this in mind, we need to make use of all the talents that parents have, and encourage them to take part fully in the life of the school. This will only happen with active and open engagement with parents, and by focusing on the creation of excellence in all that children do.

Working with parents can also reduce expenses for the science department. The joint ASE, Planet Science and NCPTA initiative to demonstrate how PTAs can support their science departments by collaborating more effectively to enhance students' motivation and learning is a good example of this. They compiled a list of 'most wanted' pieces of innovative science equipment in consultation with science teachers. They then negotiated discounts with various suppliers on specific pieces of equipment. Further information is available from the following organisations:

- ASE (The Association for Science Education): www.ase.org.uk

- Planet Science: www.planet-science.com

- NESTA (The National Endowment for Science, Technology and the Arts): www.nesta.org.uk

- NCPTA (The National Confederation of Parent Teacher Associations): www.ncpta.org.uk

- The BA (The British Association for the Advancement of Science): www.the-ba.net

However, contact with parents is usually about the individual parent's child or children. When support from parents is at a low ebb, teachers must find ways of encouraging them in to school. The following is an example of how this can be achieved.

Case study – Working with parents

Working with parents was identified as a priority for a large secondary school. The G&T coordinator recognised that there was a need for effective home–school partnerships in order to address the inbuilt underachievement of the more able students.

   The assumption of a lot of staff was that parents would not attend evening sessions. This was based on parents' evening attendance figures – unless it was a prize-giving evening. It was decided that the launch evening would have a 'celebration of success' flavour. The following actions were planned:

- Developing Excellence launch evening
- Year 8 parents brain-based learning workshops
- Year 10 home learning kit
- Year 7 Learning Styles Conference (including a special parents' workshop).

Developing Excellence launch evening:

The launch evening was a high-profile, whole-school event including staff, governors and senior management. A well-respected researcher was the keynote speaker. To ensure a relaxed and positive atmosphere there was a buffet and orchestral accompaniment. The evening was an excellent launch to the G&T initiative and was well received by parents, teachers and students. This meeting was a starting point and not the only vehicle for involving parents in the G&T strand.

Year 8 parents brain-based learning workshops:

It was recognised that a lot of parents wanted to support their children, but lacked the skills and understanding of how to effectively support their child throughout their secondary education. Parents also felt that they did not understand the content of courses offered at school. This had a detrimental effect on their confidence in communicating with their child about their academic education. They would all too often relate success at school to attendance, behaviour and punctuality, as they were confident in addressing these issues.

A brain-based learning programme for Year 8 gifted and talented students was started. Parents were encouraged to know the techniques we were using in school, so they could encourage the same strategies to be used for homework and revision. There was a workshop for Year 8 parents that covered:

- revision strategies
- use of colour
- spider gram templates/mind mapping
- use of music
- creating a supportive learning environment at home
- homework planning.

In order to maximise parental attendance, these workshops formed part of the Year 8 target-setting review day.

Year 10 home learning kit:

It was clear from conversations at parents' evenings that parents were unsure what resources were required for effective revision and where to get them. A bag full of useful materials for home learning was prepared. It included:

- A4 paper
- Blu Tack
- coloured felt pens
- small index cards
- a revision planning grid
- useful web addresses and online support
- the school's out-of-hours revision programme.

This kit was given to every parent who attended the Year 10 parents' home learning evening.

Year 7 Learning Styles Conference:

The Year 7 gifted and talented cohort was invited to a full-day conference at the Earth Centre. They spent the day developing an understanding of how they learn and how to improve it. The school's learning mentor team delivered the whole day. An important part of the conference was a parents' workshop on learning styles. This was an afternoon session covering:

- preferred learning styles – both their own and their child's
- the implications of this in how their child tackles homework and revision

> • how to develop their weaker learning styles.
>
> Parents valued the input from the school and developed closer links with staff in a non-threatening environment. The learning mentors, also part of the Excellence in Cities strand, made effective links with parents too.

How do we know if parents are supporting us?

- There is sustained interest through high attendance at parents' evenings, provides some evidence of success.

- The dialogue between parents and the school continues.

- Parents feel comfortable about coming in to school and asking questions.

- Parents attend the governors' meetings.

- Parents are kept informed about gifted and talented activities and their own children.

- Parents' improved understanding supports their children.

- Parents of able students join and/or support the PTA.

- Examination results improve.

- Parents are willing to discuss their child's progress formally and informally.

- Parents support and/or attend out-of-hours activities.

- Students are happy to attend out-of-hours activities.

- The role of gifted and talented coordinator is known and recognised by parents.

Continuing to involve parents

Barriers to parental involvement are not based on a lack of understanding but lack of opportunity and knowledge. We must find ways of listening to parents without being patronising. If other sectors in education, such as early years provision, quite openly advocate partnership with parents we should find new ways of doing this, incorporating it into our planning. Our gifted science students represent only 10% of our school cohort so we should be able to keep parents informed, whether through a generic termly newsletter, telephone conversation, or individually prepared letters reflecting the activities, opportunities and learning experienced by their children. Additionally, many parents access school websites and this is increasingly being used by schools to keep parents informed. However, it is essential that information on the website is updated regularly to maintain the interest.

We need to listen to parents too if they are really going to help us. When a parent wants to discuss their child or raise concerns we need to listen and ask them for their ideas. Schools, through the use of educational jargon and perceived elitism, raise barriers to cooperation and trust. We need to find ways to reduce some of these barriers.

Beyond the classroom

- Educational visits
- Competitions
- Summer schools
- Masterclasses
- Links with universities, business and other organisations
- Homework

Educational visits

Introduction

Science education offers the teacher a wide range of opportunities for challenging pupils to use different cognitive skills. However, taking part in educational visits challenges pupils to develop a range of social skills that are essential if the able child is to communicate effectively with their peers, mentors and the wider community. Social interaction is a normal and expected outcome on an educational visit; it can also be directed, encouraged, targeted or left to develop once catalysed. Remember to be clear in your own mind of the desired outcome of a visit and to communicate this to the pupils. Are they sure of what is expected of them? Do they understand the objectives, possible outcomes and timescales?

Planning your visit

Good planning is essential for a successful educational science visit. The pre-visit inspection not only alerts staff to any possible dangers (see the section on risk assessment below) but also gives you an opportunity to speak to centre staff. Artefacts, displays and resource materials that are not normally on show can then be requested. A focus for the visit can be established. Centre staff can be alerted as to the level of ability of the pupils attending the visit and they will be able to pitch their presentation – and any questions – at an appropriate level. This will help to maintain the pupils' interest from the start and will encourage the development of more conceptualised thinking, the application of ideas into unfamiliar circumstances, the synthesis of seemingly unrelated concepts and the reasoning out of misconceptions.

Failing to make adequate or appropriate plans can have consequences. Below is an account by one teacher of a visit to an observatory by a group of 14-year-old pupils. There were 60 pupils on the visit from five secondary schools.

We had planned as much as we thought fit. I was excited about taking our brightest pupils out on a Saturday morning because I was keen to get to know them better as individuals, you know, out of the constraints of the classroom. I had spoken to the observatory staff over the phone and told them to pitch the talk on gravity at Level 7, in preparation for their SATs. I was delighted when they said that they could get a lecturer from the astrophysics department of the university to come and speak to the pupils, show them some slides of galaxies and explain how important gravity is.

After a short walk around the observatory we entered the lecture theatre for the talk. The lecturer quickly got onto ideas about seeing stars and curved space. He started telling us about how light could be bent by gravity. The pupils looked confused. They soon switched off. Everything they had learned so far about light and gravity didn't seem to make sense.

With hindsight it is easy to criticise this teacher for not planning appropriately. It is easy now to see that the teacher knew what *they* wanted to *learn* and the lecturer knew what *he* wanted to *teach*. How could this have been better planned?

- Visit, fax or post sample SATs questions.

- Ask for a transcript of the lecture notes prior to visit.

Planning your visit should ensure that pupils are challenged to develop their scientific understanding further, not undermine their learning so far. In this context the idea of discovery learning would seem most suitable.

Planning a visit may also include deciding on groupings. You may wish to consider the following options:

- a group of able pupils in a year group in school

- a group of able pupils across two or three year groups in school

- groups of able pupils (as above) across two or three similar schools

- groups of able pupils (as above) across a network of several schools

- a group of able pupils across school phases: Years 6/7, 9/10, 11/12 in one or more schools.

Also consider the balance of pupils based on gender, ethnicity and religion. Remember that some theories we teach as science teachers directly negate the teachings of many faiths. Be sensitive to this and plan for any possible conflicts of interest that may arise from a visit. These could be outlined to parents in any initial pre-visit acceptance letter.

Thorough knowledge of the place to be visited allows for worksheets to be prepared that will stimulate interest prior to going. These should be completed in the two weeks leading up to a visit. This allows for completion of tasks, assessment of prior learning, any misconceptions to be ironed out and some negotiated targets to be set.

Prior to a visit the teacher should meet with the pupils at a convenient time for discussions about objectives, possible outcomes and when these should be achieved by.

Development of the whole child

One might assume that an able child is able to do anything. Yet often when it comes to socialising, mixing in groups or having to speak to an adult there is a lack of ability. This is why organising activities with like-minded individuals can be so successful for the able science student. They can share a common interest which gives common ground on which to talk. Able pupils may find it hard to relate to other pupils their own age simply because they feel that either they stand out or the other pupils do not measure up intellectually. Communicating their area of interest can become awkward. They may find it easier to be a quiet companion.

If you place a group of able pupils who do not know each other together they will naturally feel nervous. So, at the start of a visit, group students and present them with a few reasonably straightforward tasks requiring thought and discussion. Some examples of visit starter activities are given below (answers at the end of the chapter):

- If you catch ten flies in a jar, replace the lid and then weigh it, will the jar change weight when the flies settle on the bottom or when they fly around?

- If you dangle a large magnet in front of an iron car, will the car move?

- What will happen to the level in a bath brim-full of cold water, with a large ice boulder floating in it, when the ice melts?

- A man on a barge carrying scrap iron through the lock of a canal throws a large piece of iron into the sealed lock. What happens to the water level?

Now only give each student in the group one answer and ask them to explain the answer to the other members of the group. It must be noted at this stage that while all the pupils present may be able to discuss science problems with ease, they should be encouraged to spend time together also discussing themselves, their own interests and hobbies. This could be the focus of the lunchtime activities – tell the group a little bit about the person on your left, favourite television show, radio station, etc.

Post-visit activities

No visit is useful in contributing to the academic attainment of a pupil unless the features of the visit are embedded in the curriculum. It is essential that the content of what was learned is evaluated and assessed. This may be in the form of an improved score in a unit test or modular exam. To develop this idea further, teachers should strive to look at the processes involved in the learning and teach the pupils to apply those to other areas of the science curriculum. Let us look at a case study of a trip to a water treatment plant.

Year 8 water treatment plant visit – activities upon returning to school

After visiting the plant and seeing the stages of water treatment, the teacher assessed the pupils' learning by also including some additional SATs questions onto the end of the unit test for microbes and disease. The pupils were able to demonstrate their understanding of the role of saprophytic bacteria in the making of compost.

The teacher met with the pupils a few days later to discuss how they had been able to interpret the role of these bacteria in different circumstances. The pupils had examined flow charts at the water treatment plant showing the stages in the cleaning of sewage. They had found the flow chart method, like mind mapping, a useful tool in visualising what was going on. By making the process easy they were able to focus on the role of individual elements of the breakdown of waste – the types of bacteria, giving the waste a large surface area, the bubbling of oxygen.

In the next unit of work on rocks, the teacher asked the pupils to use the method of flow charts, which would enable the pupils to focus on the fine detail of the unit.

Risk assessment

Safety on educational visits is of primary and utmost importance. Thankfully, the number of fatalities on educational visits is very small. Each year, it is estimated that across England there are 7–10 million pupil visits involving educational and/or recreational activity. On average, there are 3–4 fatalities. The vast majority of visits are carried out safely and responsibly, and they provide quality learning experiences for young people, giving them opportunities for a broader education, and they provide an excellent opportunity for young people to meet like-minded individuals.

Organisers of visits have a responsibility to ensure that they are properly planned and carried out. Provided that organisers do a proper risk assessment and take all reasonably practicable measures to deal with the identified risks, the scope for incidents occurring in the first place should be minimised. The DfES produces comprehensive guidance for people who organise such visits, to enable them to set up systems and procedures that better support teachers and others leading visits. This is found on the websites www.teachernet.gov.uk/visits and www.standards.dfes.gov.uk. Additional to this are a range of publications. The DfEE (1998) guidance document *Health and Safety of Pupils on Educational Visits: A Good Practice Guide (HASPEV)* and three-part supplement (2002) are useful references.

There are many people working in education who have a great deal of expertise in running visits safely. If you are planning a visit then it would be good practice to ask them to share their knowledge with you. All schools should now have an educational visits coordinator (EVC), and they can also provide advice, direction and, most importantly, the relevant forms to fill in. Most LAs are drawing up generic risk assessments for frequently used types of visit to reduce the workload on schools. Many LAs are sharing these assessments with each other. Check with your own EVC and LA for the required forms and documentation for your school. In the meantime, a generic blank risk assessment form is provided on the accompanying website, which should enable you to start planning an activity, but ensure you use your own school forms for the visit.

Here are some handy hints about what to do when considering an educational visit:

- Follow the guidance.

- Conduct the risk assessment – the essential risk management tool.

- Plan properly, including contingency planning for the unexpected.

- Check that the safety arrangements work properly in practice.

- It is realistic for organisers to do risk assessment, it is plain common sense to anticipate problems and plan what to do about them.

- Share all the information with your senior manager and head teacher.

Educational employers must be satisfied that their teachers are competent to lead or supervise a visit. The DfES guidance package sets out what training is appropriate for the type of visit. The Health and Safety at Work Act 1974 places overall responsibility for health and safety with the employer. In many cases, the employer will be the local authority. In other cases, it will be the school that will be the employer. Guidance explaining who is responsible for the health and safety of school staff, pupils and others on school premises or when engaged on educational activities including visits is available in the DfES publication *Health and Safety: Responsibilities and Powers* (2001).

> This additional guidance will help members thinking about taking part in such activities to become aware of the range and complexity of the issues that must be taken into account in the planning of educational visits.
>
> (NASUWT)

Health and safety law has for a long time placed responsibility for controlling risk on those best placed to do so – those who create the risk in the first place. Teachers and organisers who act responsibly by following good practice need not fear prosecution if an accident happens.

Keeping parents informed

Parents should expect all school trips for their children to be well organised. Parents should feel free to ask questions – about contingency planning, about knowledge, skills and qualifications of those leading the trips, about standards which will be followed and about risk assessment. Parents should expect schools to provide information on these topics. This can be done via a letter sent to parents, particularly if it is a short day trip locally. The letter should outline times, places to visit, modes of transport, accompanying staff and a reply slip for parental permission. This also gives parents the opportunity to write back with questions. Parents should feel secure about contacting the school to ask questions.

For activities further afield, those with greater risk (such as those involving water) and residential activities, the parents should ideally be invited in to school to discuss arrangements.

Other useful information, particularly for group leaders, can be found in the three supplements to *HASPEV* (DfEE 1998), which are *Standards for LEAs in Overseeing Educational Visits*, *Standards for Adventure* and *A Handbook for Group Leaders*, all published in 2002 by the DfES, and in *Health and Safety: Responsibilities and Powers* (DfES 2001).

Competitions

Each year you will find a raft of science competitions being launched for schools. Some are specific for that year and some are annual events that schools regularly participate in. In this section you will find just a small selection, taken from a search on the internet, that schools can access to engage, enrich and extend the more able students. The selection is designed to entice you into finding something for your own school by looking for something yourself, rather than recommending a particular organisation or competition.

The Biotechnology and Biological Sciences Research Council

The BBSRC is the UK's principal funder of biological research and it supports research and research training in universities and research centres throughout the UK. It promotes knowledge transfer from research to applications in business, industry and policy, as well as public engagement in the biosciences. The BBSRC was established by royal charter in 1994 by incorporation of the former Agricultural and Food Research Council with the biotechnology and biological sciences programmes of the former Science and Engineering Research Council.

The BBSRC funds research in some of the most exciting areas of contemporary science, including:

● genomics, stem cell biology, and bionanotechnology, which provide a basis for new technologies in healthcare, food safety, plant and livestock breeding, and bioprocessing

- whole-organism biology relevant to our understanding of diet and health, ageing, animal health and welfare, infectious diseases and immunity, and crop productivity

- biological populations and systems that underpin agricultural sustainability, biodiversity and novel bio-based and renewable processes for energy and manufacturing.

The competitions are designed to be a lead-in for students to engage them in this line of education and research. The Council has organised many successful poster competitions for schools. Topics have ranged from illustrating the importance of the work of Alexander Fleming and Louis Pasteur to encouraging children to think about the causes of illness and how to avoid them. The judges were looking for the scientific accuracy of the facts and for eye-catching presentations, and they definitely found both! The BBSRC has teamed up with other organisations such as the Department for Environment, Food and Rural Affairs (Defra) (formerly MAFF) to challenge students to produce models and short films about various topics. Dr John Sherlock from MAFF and Tracey Reader from the BBSRC ended up in the Creepy Crawly Gallery of the Natural History museum where they presented awards to the winners of a Design an Insect competition. The challenge was to develop an insect that would be an effective pollinator, but each category had a specific aim. The 5- to 7-year-olds looked at the importance of the wings in helping the insect to move from place to place, 8- to 9-year-olds designed a specific feature that would help in the pollination process and 10- to 12-year-olds developed a working model that demonstrated how the insect actually collected and deposited the pollen.

More details about the BBSRC's schools and community activities are available at www.bbsrc.ac.uk/society/schools.

The Institute of Biology

A range of competitions based around the biological sciences can be found at the Institute of Biology's website at www.iob.org.

The Royal Society of Chemistry

For competitions with a chemistry flavour, try the Royal Society of Chemistry (www.rsc.org). The RSC is the largest organisation in Europe for advancing the chemical sciences. Supported by a worldwide network of members and an international publishing business, their activities span education, conferences, science policy and the promotion of chemistry to the public.

The Schools' Analyst Competition is a national competition run by the RSC's Analytical Division for first-year sixth form or equivalent. Analytical Division Regions hold heats to select a team to go through to the national final. Each team comprises three students. Teams are required to undertake various practical analytical determinations based on problems relevant to industrial or social needs. These are judged for skill, understanding and accuracy and are intended to promote teamwork and safety in the laboratory. Each competition aims to provide some tasks which are relatively familiar to the students, such as titrations, and others which are likely to be unfamiliar, such as chromatographic separations or atomic and molecular spectroscopy. In this way, it is hoped that the competitors will learn new skills, as well as demonstrate their existing knowledge and skills.

The Royal Astronomical Society

The physical sciences are vast and diverse, but the Royal Astronomical Society (RAS) offers an extensive range of competitions often based around literacy activities. The Society is the UK's leading professional body for astronomy and astrophysics, geophysics, solar and solar–terrestrial physics, and planetary sciences, and organises scientific meetings and publishes research and review journals. The Society also awards grants and prizes, maintains an extensive library and supports educational activities.

A recent RAS competition had the title 'Global warming makes the headlines every day!' The task was to write about the causes and effects of global warming and to be critical of the reports and evidence found. The school pupils had to create a newspaper or write a feature article to discuss and criticise this topical subject.

The RAS's highly successful interdisciplinary competitions have been run for the last eight years, and are an excellent opportunity to forge cross-curricular links and to use the internet and the library to search for material.

Planet Science

There is a wide range of interesting competitions and activities on the Planet Science website at www.planet-science.com. This website started life as the public face of the DfES's Science Year project, which was then extended and renamed Planet Science.

Science clubs

As well as competitions, it is always helpful to have science clubs for the more able students. The benefits include peer support, extension work on current learning, enrichment and development of social skills, support for the students if they are not receiving adequate support at home, and a chance to promote the subject across the school. You can find lots of useful information on setting up and running a science club, in collaboration with a local science centre for support and advice, at www.scizmic.net. sciZmic, the science discovery clubs network, links together science clubs, science centres and partner organisations. There are many organisations supporting science clubs, so log on and find out more about how they could support your club.

Summer schools

There are several ways of getting your most able students into a summer school, and the various types in the UK are discussed below.

Your own summer school

Often there is not the time within the constraints of the national curriculum to do a lot of the interesting practical science activities that you would like to do. Organising a summer school can give you that opportunity, in a relaxed atmosphere where achievement rather than attainment can be celebrated. Here are some points to consider when organising your own summer school for able students:

- How many students will you invite?

- You will need at least two staff, plus technician support.

- Organise for a teacher/TA to come in to give you a break each day.

- You need parental consent forms and medical forms.

- Compile up-to-date emergency contact numbers.

- Order equipment and photocopying in advance.

- Check that school systems will be operating.

- Check costings, including school room hire.

- Obtain consent from the head teacher and the governors.

The type of summer school you organise will depend on your own strengths. Whatever you decide to focus on, you can do it in a variety of ways:

- Design, plan and build something, e.g. a chemical rocket, a wild pond or a model.

- Research something, e.g. the local habitat, fitness, web-based research.

- Conduct a practical investigation of something, e.g. material strengths, electrical efficiency.

- Act out something like the discovery of penicillin, a model of electrical resistance, the life of a scientist.

- Make a film, e.g. using time-lapse photography, to record practical investigations for future use and for coursework.

It is important that all students take part and thus a mixture of all the above approaches can be used. Develop the strengths found amongst the students, involve them in the planning, give them ownership, and most of all celebrate their success by having an achievement ceremony at the end of the week. Invite parents to come along, present certificates, display what has been done, and ask the students to reflect on what they have done and what they have learned. This evaluation will help them apply their learning when they return to school for normal lessons.

Excellence Cluster/G&T Network summer schools

If you are thinking of putting on a summer school but find it is too costly, then approach your Learning Network coordinator. They receive additional funding to help with collaborative activities. This may be with a particular year group, getting like-minded and similarly able students together to study science-related activities, or even like-minded staff who want to share expertise with staff in other schools. Alternatively, it could be that you wish to organise a transition summer school for Year 6 and Year 7 students, allowing the transition from Key Stage 2 to Key Stage 3 to run a little more smoothly. Remember, this can be a good way of winning over your new recruits for September and turning them on to science. Make sure you have additional activities for the more able students when they arrive in September, such as a science club, to keep the interest going.

Local university summer schools

Develop close links with the local providers of further and higher education. Many university science departments are keen to develop links, as the student who visits in Year 10 or 11 may then return to study after they leave school. It is also possible that they will provide used equipment for your department when they upgrade their own facilities.

A quick search through the university websites will reveal a range of opportunities, or consult your school's Aimhigher coordinator, whose role is to encourage students in Year 9 through to Year 13 to go to university. Many universities receive central funding to put on these summer schools, to help the government achieve its target of getting 50% of students leaving school to go to university.

The summer schools are varied and may focus on the particular strengths of the department. They are a good way for students to find out if their favourite science topic is adequately provided for at the particular university.

One such summer school is the Black Science Summer School at Hope University in Liverpool. It encourages students from African and Caribbean families to study forensic science, whilst also letting them get a flavour of university life.

YG&T (formerly NAGTY) summer schools

The National Academy for Gifted and Talented Youth (NAGTY) was based at the University of Warwick in Coventry from 2002. It has now been replaced by the

Young, Gifted & Talented (YGT) programme, managed by CfBT Education Trust. You can find out more about becoming a member at www.ygt.dcsf.gov.uk/

NAGTY summer schools were a firmly established feature of the educational portfolio available to able students. In March 2004 Ofsted published a very positive report of the 2003 summer schools, drawing out the extent to which they impacted on members' educational and social development. Early research showed that from the 2004 summer schools the educational impact on participants actually increases over time and is even greater when they return to school.

In 2004, the summer schools on offer at Imperial College were based around space research, with a focus on the Mars mission. Students learned about superconducting materials, Mars Rover robotics and the geology of Mars, as well as general astronomy. Details of YGT summer schools and activities are available on their website.

Other summer schools

In 2005, for the first time, the University of Leeds hosted a Salters' Chemistry Camp, which was held in the colour chemistry department. For this camp the Salters' Institute worked in partnership with the Clothworkers' Company and the Dyers' Company. The camp was additionally supported by the Armourers and Brasiers' Company and the Company of Merchant Adventurers of the City of York.

Fifty students spent five days participating in colour chemistry activities in the university laboratories. During the activities the students got the opportunity to investigate chemiluminescence of 'cold light' and to find out what makes fireflies glow, and they had fun with dyes and dyeing and could practise using dyes for printing. These activities were supported by a site visit to a local chemical plant. There were also social activities in the evening which included tenpin bowling and a sports evening.

Further information on the Salters' Chemistry Camps is available at www.chemistrycamps.co.uk.

Masterclasses

The difference between a masterclass and any other activity is that you would normally involve outside speakers, teachers, lecturers and professionals from the science workplace to give a different feel to the day.

You can use your local SETPOINT to get access to a range of professionals, from business, industry, charities, governmental agencies, educational organisations and institutions. Ensure that you have good dialogue with the speakers before they come in. They need to know:

- number of pupils

- age of pupils

- gender mix

- ability of pupils

- prior learning

- expected learning outcomes

- language levels.

Here are some ideas for a masterclass in your school:

- Uses of enzymes for Year 10. This could be delivered by the production manager from a local food processing plant or chemical factory.

- Principle of moments for Year 9. Use the engineering department at your local university.

- Uses of plastics for Year 10. Ask the owner of a local double glazing business about production, use and disposal of plastics.

- Adaptations of animals for Year 7. Contact staff from the local zoo, farm or veterinary surgery.

- Plant anatomy for Year 8. Invite staff from the local parks department or garden centre.

- Recycling for Year 7. Ask staff from local charitable organisations.

The possibilities are endless, and the masterclasses can take place either outside of school, within school during science club, or within lessons.

Links with universities, business and other organisations

When developing links with the community, a first port of call could be your regional SETPOINT organisations. These bridge the gap between education and business and they will be able to offer competitions, advice, funding for CREST awards and links into business and industry. Your local representative can be contacted through the Science, Engineering, Technology, and Mathematics Network (SETNET) website at www.setnet.org.uk. This will put you in touch with a huge range of educational organisations, institutions, professions, charities, businesses, industries and government bodies. The full list is available on the SETNET website and a copy is included on the accompanying website.

Each year the SETPOINT regional organisations offer a diverse range of activities, all of which inspire able students. The extract below is from the Greater Merseyside SETPOINT newsletter, 2003.

GETSET 2003

GETSET stands for Girls Entering Tomorrow's Science, Engineering and Technology. The aim of the event is to excite young women about science, engineering and technology. Independent evaluation of the programme has stated that it is directly linked to generating positive attitudes towards SET careers amongst young women. GETSET women are 3.5 times more likely than their peers to pursue A level physics and 2.5 times more likely to pursue maths or chemistry.

Once again Merseyside SETPOINT held their annual October GETSET at Liverpool Football Club. 450 Year 9 girls descended upon Anfield over a three day period to take part in the challenge. The girls were divided into teams of 8 with a mentor from industry in order to save the day.

The scenario was that Liverpool Football Club had been taken over by rival supporters. The team were being held hostage and the girls had to carry out a number of tasks in order to save them. The tasks included making a cart from dexion which could be driven by a player, designing and making a bridge from plumber's piping that could be used to escape, producing an alarm using electronic circuits, building bivouacs for shelter, and much more.

Projects such as these place students in situations where they learn to work as members of a team and where skills other than scientific ones are developed – communication, presentation, personal effectiveness and so on.

Your local SETPOINT can help you make contact with a range of organisations, for example The Royal Society of Chemistry. The RSC is the largest non-governmental supporter of chemistry education in the UK, and their activities include:

- curriculum material that is sent free to all schools and colleges in the UK

- events such as Chemistry at Work, which is aimed at giving students an idea of how chemistry and chemical science is used in everyday life through presentations, demonstrations and hands-on activities

- in-service training courses for teachers, including industry study tours, management workshops and ICT workshops

- a comprehensive careers advice service in chemistry for both teachers and students.

Detailed information on all RSC education products and activities is available on the website at www.chemsoc.org/learnnet.

Homework

The impact of parental involvement in raising children's education attainment has long been established. In order to gain the benefits of parent partnerships with homework, however, consideration should be given to points discussed below.

Open dialogue is essential

Parents need to understand why their support is required as many believe that they should let teachers get on with things and so do not get involved. You may need to plan a range of initiatives to explain to as many parents/carers as possible what you are proposing to do for their gifted child. This may include a range of strategies such as personalised letters, specially organised meetings (considering venues other than the school) and activities involving teachers, pupils and parents.

Overcome barriers to support

It is essential that we assure parents that it is the time that they give to their children that is important, and the supportive dialogue that encourages their children. Parents can ask their children how they felt about a homework task, what worked well for them in tackling a piece of homework, which piece of music helped them to focus while being creative. Parents can ask for a rating out of 10: 'How challenging did you feel that homework was?' or 'How well did you tackle that problem?' Parents just need to know how to support, not what the answers to the homework tasks are. Simple explanatory notes with examples are sometimes all that is required to assist parents in engaging with their children and supporting with homework tasks. This could be in the form of a sheet explaining some higher order thinking verbs, for example:

- **Explain – say what is happening and give a reason.** Use the word 'because' to make sure you have explained. For example, if asked to explain why you take a tablet for indigestion, you would answer: 'Indigestion is caused by a build-up of acid in the stomach. The acid needs to be neutralised. The opposite of an acid is an alkali, so when I have a tablet it gets rid of the indigestion because the alkali tablet will neutralise the acid.'

- **Compare and contrast – comment on the similarities and differences between two or more things.** If asked to do this for animals and plants, you would answer: 'Both living things carry out the seven life processes (MRS GREN), but plants make their own food whilst animals consume food.'

- **Analyse – look for patterns, trends or unusual things in a set of results or other information.** If asked to do this for the different light bulbs in your house, you would answer: 'As the wattage of the bulb increases the brightness increases, the cost of using the bulb increases, but there is also a lot more heat, which is a waste of energy. This does depend on the type of light bulb because certain bulbs are designed to use less electricity. I can only analyse light bulbs of the same type.'

Supporting the unsupported child

Unfortunately, there may be a small number of pupils who do not get the required help. This may be due to a number of issues. However, support may be given through a science homework club, or the pupil might complete the homework with peer support. Allow them into the department at lunchtime or before school.

Do not overburden parents

It is essential not to be too demanding of the parents' goodwill for it can easily be withdrawn. Give consideration to how frequently homework tasks are set, and the type of homework being set. Keep up the parents' interest and motivation by varying the tasks, from research, to creative writing, to data analysis. Parents may then start to feed back the type of tasks most enjoyed by the student, the type of task that was most challenging, and, most importantly, those tasks that disengage the student. Consult teachers in other departments about the demands they place upon parents and consider how this may have a negative effect on the student.

Evaluate the homework activities with the pupil and parents

This can be done through the use of homework diaries, record sheets or even the pupil's exercise books when marking is completed. Problems need to be reviewed and successes need to be celebrated. A meeting can also be arranged to listen to the views of the parents and this can help to consolidate your working practices.

Reward the commitment and it will be sustained

At the end of each half term, letters to parents should be sent. They can be standard letters of thanks but when received by parents, addressed to them about their child, they become very personal. This means a lot to parents and will help them to feel valued as contributors to their child's education and improve communication between school and parents. This can also give the homework activities a higher profile. Acknowledging the homework responses through assemblies, the school website and newsletter and displays can also help.

Homework reinforces education as a 'shared responsibility' between home and school

Homework can provide the ideal vehicle for establishing such a working partnership. Parents need to be aware that the input they make out of school has a significant impact on their child's performance in school. The assistance of parents and carers is therefore essential to ensure that pupils perform to the best of their ability.

Answers to visit starter activities (as if you needed them)

- **Flies** – the jar will weigh the same. The weight depends on the mass in the jar and that does not change. When the fly is in the air, currents transfer the force to the bottom of the jar. Friction slows the air currents down at the bottom of the jar so that the air currents hitting the top of the jar have a smaller force.

- **Car/magnet** – the car will not move. Newton's Third Law explains that the force on the car is equal and opposite to the force on the magnet.

- **Ice water** – the water level will stay exactly the same. The weight of the water displaced by the ice boulder exactly equals the weight of the ice boulder. When the ice boulder melts it 'shrinks' and turns back to water and fits exactly into the volume of water it displaced.

- **Iron/barge** – when the iron was on the barge it displaced an amount of water equal to its weight, which is about five times its volume. When thrown into the water it only displaces its volume. So the level of water in the lock goes down.

Appendices

Institutional quality standards in gifted and talented education

Generic Elements	Entry	Developing	Exemplary
	A – Effective teaching and learning strategies		
1. Identification	i. The school/college has learning conditions and systems to identify gifted and talented pupils in all year groups and an agreed definition and shared understanding of the meaning of 'gifted and talented' within its own, local and national contexts.	i. Individual pupils are screened annually against clear criteria at school/college and subject/topic level.	i. **Multiple criteria and sources of evidence** are used to identify gifts and talents, including through the use of a broad range of quantitative and qualitative data.
	ii. An **accurate record** of the identified gifted and talented population is kept and updated.	ii. The record is used to identify under-achievement and **exceptional achievement** (both within and outside the population) and to track/review pupil **progress**.	ii. The record is supported by a comprehensive monitoring, progress planning and reporting system which all staff regularly share and contribute to.
	iii. The identified gifted and talented population broadly reflects the school/college's **social and economic composition**, gender and ethnicity.	iii. **Identification** systems address issues of **multiple exceptionality** (pupils with specific gifts/talents and special educational needs).	iii. **Identification** processes are regularly reviewed and refreshed in the light of pupil performance and value-added data. The gifted and talented population is fully representative of the school/college's population.
Evidence			
Next steps			
2. Effective provision in the classroom	i. The school/college addresses the different needs of the gifted and talented population by providing a stimulating learning environment and by extending the teaching repertoire.	i. Teaching and learning strategies are diverse and flexible, meeting the needs of distinct pupil groups within the gifted and talented population (e.g. able underachievers, exceptionally able).	i. The school/college has established a range of methods to find out what works best in the classroom, and shares this within the school/college and with other schools and colleges.
	ii. Teaching and learning is differentiated and delivered through both individual and group activities.	ii. A range of challenging learning and teaching strategies is evident in lesson planning and delivery. **Independent learning** skills are developed.	ii. Teaching and learning are suitably challenging and varied, incorporating the **breadth, depth** and **pace** required to progress high achievement. Pupils routinely work independently and self-reliantly.

	iii. Opportunities exist to extend learning through **new technologies**.	iii. The use of **new technologies** across the curriculum is focused on **personalised learning** needs.	iii. The innovative use of **new technologies** raises the achievement and motivation of gifted and talented pupils.
Evidence			
Next steps			
3. Standards	i. Levels of **attainment** and **achievement** for gifted and talented pupils are comparatively high in relation to the rest of the school/college population and are in line with those of similar pupils in similar schools/colleges.	i. Levels of **attainment** and **achievement** for gifted and talented pupils are broadly consistent across the gifted and talented population and above those of similar pupils in similar schools/colleges.	i. Levels of attainment and achievement for gifted and talented pupils indicate sustainability over time and are well above those of similar pupils in similar schools/colleges.
	ii. Self-evaluation indicates that gifted and talented provision is satisfactory.	ii. Self-evaluation indicates that gifted and talented provision is good.	ii. Self-evaluation indicates that gifted and talented provision is very good or excellent.
	iii. Schools/colleges' gifted and talented education programmes are explicitly linked to the achievement of SMART outcomes and these highlight improvements in pupils' attainment and achievement.		
Evidence			
Next steps			

B – Enabling curriculum entitlement and choice

4. Enabling curriculum entitlement and choice	i. The curriculum offers opportunities and guidance to pupils which enable them to work beyond their age and/or phase, and across subjects or topics, according to their aptitudes and interests.		i. The curriculum offers **personalised learning pathways** for pupils which maximise individual **potential**, retain flexibility of future choices, extend well beyond test/examination requirements and result in sustained impact on pupil **attainment and achievement.**
Evidence			
Next steps			

Definitions for words and phrases in bold are provided in the glossary in the Quality Standards *User Guide*, available at www2.teachernet.gov.uk/gat.

Generic Elements	Entry	Developing	Exemplary
C – Assessment for learning			
5. Assessment for learning	i. Processes of data analysis and pupil assessment are employed throughout the school/college to plan learning for gifted and talented pupils.	i. Routine progress reviews, using both qualitative and quantitative data, make effective use of prior, predictive and value-added **attainment** data to plan for progression in pupils' learning.	i. **Assessment data** are used by teachers and across the school/college to ensure challenge and sustained progression in individual pupils' learning.
	ii. Dialogue with pupils provides focused feedback which is used to plan future learning.	ii. Systematic oral and written feedback helps pupils to set challenging curricular targets.	ii. Formative assessment and individual target setting combine to maximise and celebrate pupils' achievements.
	iii. Self and peer assessment, based on clear understanding of criteria, are used to increase pupils' responsibility for learning.	iii. Pupils reflect on their own skill development and are involved in the design of their own targets and tasks.	iii. Classroom practice regularly requires pupils to reflect on their own **progress** against targets, and engage in the direction of their own learning.
Evidence			
Next steps			
6. Transfer and transition	i. Shared processes, using agreed criteria, are in place to ensure the productive transfer of information from one setting to another (i.e. from class to class, year to year and school/college to school/college).	i. Transfer information concerning gifted and talented pupils, including parental input, informs targets for pupils to ensure **progress** in learning. Particular attention is given to including new admissions.	i. Transfer data concerning gifted and talented pupils are used to inform planning of teaching and learning at subject/aspect/topic and individual pupil level, and to ensure progression according to ability rather than age or phase.
Evidence			
Next steps			
D – School/college organisation			
7. Leadership	i. A named member of the governing body, senior management team and the lead professional responsible for gifted and talented education have clearly directed responsibilities for motivating and driving gifted and talented provision. The head teacher actively champions gifted and talented provision.	i. **Responsibility** for gifted and talented provision is **distributed**, and evaluation of its impact shared, at all levels in the school/college. Staff subscribe to policy at all levels. Governors play a significant supportive and evaluative role.	i. Organisational structures, communication channels and the deployment of staff (e.g. workforce remodelling) are flexible and creative in supporting the delivery of **personalised learning**. Governors take a lead in celebrating achievements of gifted and talented pupils.
Evidence			

8. Policy	i. The gifted and talented policy is integral to the school/college's inclusion agenda and approach to personalised learning, feeds into and from the single school/college improvement plan and is consistent with other policies.	i. The policy directs and reflects best practice in the school/college, is regularly reviewed and is clearly linked to other policy documentation.	i. The policy includes input from the whole-school/college community and is regularly refreshed in the light of innovative national and international practice.
Evidence			
Next steps			
9. School/college ethos and pastoral care	i. The school/college sets high expectations, recognises achievement and celebrates the successes of all its pupils. ii. The school/college identifies and addresses the particular social and emotional needs of gifted and talented pupils in consultation with pupils, parents and carers.	i. The school/college fosters an environment which promotes positive behaviour for learning. Pupils are listened to and their views taken into account. ii. Strategies exist to counteract bullying and any adverse effects of social and curriculum pressures. Specific support for able underachievers and pupils from different cultures and social backgrounds is available and accessible.	i. An ethos of ambition and achievement is agreed and shared by the whole school/college community. Success across a wide range of abilities is celebrated. ii. The school/college places equal emphasis on high achievement and emotional well being, underpinned by programmes of support personalised to the needs of gifted and talented pupils. There are opportunities for pupils to use their gifts to benefit other pupils and the wider community.
Evidence			
Next steps			
10. Staff development	i. Staff have received professional development in meeting the needs of gifted and talented pupils.	i. The induction programme for new staff addresses gifted and talented issues, both at whole school/college and specific subject/aspect level.	i. There is **ongoing audit of staff needs** and an appropriate range of professional development in gifted and talented education. Professional development is informed by research and collaboration within and beyond the school/college.

Definitions for words and phrases in bold are provided in the glossary in the Quality Standards *User Guide*, available at www2.teachernet.gov.uk/gat.

Generic Elements	Entry	Developing	Exemplary
	ii. The lead professional responsible for gifted and talented education has received appropriate professional development.	ii. Subject/aspect and phase leaders have received specific professional development in meeting the needs of gifted and talented pupils.	ii. Priorities for the development of gifted and talented provision are included within a professional development entitlement for all staff and are monitored through performance management processes.
Evidence			
Next steps			
11. Resources	i. Provision for gifted and talented pupils is supported by appropriate budgets and resources.	i. Allocated resources include school/college based and nationally available resources, and these have a significant and measurable impact on the progress that pupils make and their attitudes to learning.	i. Resources are used to stimulate innovative and experimental practice, which is shared throughout the school/college and which are regularly reviewed for impact and best value.
Evidence			
Next steps			
12. Monitoring and evaluation	i. **Subject and phase audits** focus on the quality of teaching and learning for gifted and talented pupils. Whole school/college targets are set using prior **attainment data.**	i. Performance against targets (including at pupil level) is regularly reviewed. Targets include qualitative pastoral and curriculum outcomes as well as numerical data.	i. Performance against targets is rigorously evaluated against clear criteria. Qualitative and quantitative outcomes inform whole-school/college self-evaluation processes.
	ii. Elements of provision are planned against clear objectives within effective whole-school self-evaluation processes.	ii. All elements, including non-academic aspects of gifted and talented provision, are planned to clear objectives and are subjected to detailed evaluation.	ii. The school/college examines and challenges its own provision to inform development of further experimental and innovative practice in collaboration with other schools/colleges.
Evidence			
Next steps			

E – Strong partnerships beyond the school

13. Engaging with the community, families and beyond	i. Parents/carers are aware of the school's/college's policy on gifted and talented provision, contribute to its **identification** processes and are kept informed of developments in gifted and talented provision, including through the School Profile.	i. Progression of gifted and talented pupils is enhanced by home-school/college partnerships. There are strategies to engage and support hard-to-reach parents/carers.	i. Parents/carers are actively engaged in extending provision. Support for gifted and talented provision is integrated with other children's services (e.g. Sure Start, EAL, traveller, refugee, **LAC** Services).
	ii. The school/college shares good practice and has some collaborative provision with other schools, colleges and the wider community.	ii. A coherent strategy for networking with other schools, colleges and local community organisations extends and enriches provision.	ii. There is strong emphasis on collaborative and innovative working with other schools/colleges which impacts on quality of provision locally, regionally and nationally.
Evidence			
Next steps			
14. Learning beyond the classroom	i. There are opportunities for pupils to learn beyond the school/college day and site (extended hours and out-of-school activities).	i. A coherent programme of enrichment and extension activities (through extended hours and out-of-school activities) complements teaching and learning and helps identify pupils' latent gifts and talents.	i. Innovative models of learning beyond the classroom are developed in collaboration with local and national schools/colleges to further enhance teaching and learning.
	ii. Pupils participate in dedicated gifted and talented activities (e.g. summer schools) and their participation is recorded.	ii. Local and national provision helps meet individual pupils' learning needs, e.g. NAGTY membership, accessing outreach, local enrichment programmes.	ii. Coherent strategies are used to direct and develop individual expert performance via external agencies, e.g. HE/FE links, online support, and local/regional/national programmes.
Evidence			
Next steps			

Definitions for words and phrases in bold are provided in the glossary in the Quality Standards *User Guide*, available at www2.teachernet.gov.uk/gat.

Policy for able students in science

Area	Content	✓
Aims	Identify, encourage, extend, enrich and celebrate the achievements of our most able pupils, in a happy, safe learning culture.	
Definitions	• gifted learners are those who have abilities in one or more subjects in the statutory school curriculum other than art, design, music, performing arts and PE • talented learners are those who have abilities in art, design, music, performing arts or PE. The DfEE defines • gifted students as more able academically • talented students as more able artistically and in performance. More able pupils may also show leadership skills and social awareness. It is important to remember that some gifted and talented pupils may also be on the SEN register or have English as an additional language.	
Identification	Our school identifies the top 10% of students. These will be classified as the gifted and talented cohort. The gifted students include those who are most able in one or more of the statutory school curriculum subjects, such as science, and account for 7% of the cohort, with the remaining 3% being talented in art, design, music, PE or performing arts. The pupils are identified using a variety of data, including Key Stage 2 and 3 SATs levels from QCA as well as teacher-assessed SATs levels, NfER, CAT, MiDYiS/YELLIS data for verbal, non-verbal and maths, Fisher Family Trust data, unit test scores/ end-of-year exam scores, attainment in scientific enquiry, performance in modular science exams at Key Stage 4, peer nomination through discussion, letters to seek parental nomination, and self-nomination through discussion.	
Science-specific guidance	Gifted science students go beyond obvious answers, relate obscure facts, explain using models, are dissatisfied with simple answers, miss out steps to problems, question others – even teachers, consider alternatives, spot patterns, have more extensive vocabulary, have mathematical skills, are bored by simple repetition, are self-critical, are careless with easy work, have intense interest in one area, and think logically, giving explanations for phenomena.	
Curriculum	The department aims to provide a stimulating and challenging curriculum with opportunities to use a variety of skills when learning, and thus: • schemes of work reflect opportunities for the most able • learning and teaching strategies encourage able students • students engage in lessons using higher order thinking skills • strategies are developed for more able students to take GCSE examinations early • the school homework policy will be used with all students although staff provide appropriate homework for the more able • resources reflect the needs of the most able.	
Differentiation	The department recognises that able students are all different and so strives to provide a quality learning and teaching environment for all able students regardless of: • literacy level • learning disabilities	

Area	Content	✓
	<li> language ability (EAL)</li><li> preferred learning style (VAK)</li>so that all students can progress to their full potential.	
Data and assessment	The department uses transition data and data acquired whilst at our school to evaluate progress, set targets and monitor performance. The person responsible for able students in science collects and collates data and provides this to staff, to assist with planning provision and personalised learning, and the school coordinator. The student will have a personal progress plan compiled from available data and student/staff input. It will be effective in the following ways:<li> it will assist able students with their future planning</li><li> it will help pupils to be more aware of their particular strengths and weaknesses</li><li> the negotiated targets and objectives will encourage the students to be more focused</li><li> they will provide greater feedback to subject teachers which will aid them with lesson planning and differentiation</li><li> the personal progress plans may help to identify potential gifts and/or talents in other areas.</li>	
Grouping	<li> Students are grouped according to their ability.</li><li> A student may be accelerated if it is in their best interest, but only after consultation with the student, parents and the pastoral team.</li><li> Students are fast tracked for GCSE entry.</li>	
Links	<li> The science department develops effective links with other schools, the local community, business and industry in order to extend the science curriculum, enhance teaching and learning and develop pupils' wider understanding of science in our world.</li><li> Learning mentors support our able students and we work closely with them.</li><li> Parents are consulted and kept informed of their children's progress.</li><li> Able students may encounter peer problems, and therefore we rely upon form tutors, year heads and the school coordinator to report any problems.</li><li> Links with other departments are encouraged and each year several projects take place between departments.</li>	
Activities	<li> The department offers a range of lunchtime and after school clubs to support independent learning.</li><li> The students attend SETPOINT activities regularly.</li><li> Students benefit from visiting speakers and shows.</li><li> Each year students are offered out-of-hours activities, masterclasses and summer schools to extend and enrich their learning.</li>	
Monitoring	<li> Challenging targets are set for pupils and staff.</li><li> Monitor achievement and underachievement, and have systems in place to act on both.</li><li> The school's assessment and marking policies will be utilised as they stand, and should celebrate achievement and attainment. They should also inform students of how to make progress.</li>	
Evaluation	<li> Evaluate provision and attainment and use this information to help with subsequent planning for improvement.</li>	
Continuing professional development	<li> The person responsible for able students in science encourages continuing professional development for all staff.</li>	

The head of department's roles and responsibilities in relation to the most able students

- Subject leaders should liaise with their team in order to ensure that the most able are identified. The list of pupils should be shared with the teacher responsible for able pupils in science and the school gifted and talented coordinator.

- Subject leaders should have an up-to-date register of their most able pupils in each year group.

- Schemes of work should be developed which contain suitable enrichment and extension work and corresponding resources.

The roles and responsibilities of the coordinator for most able students

- Develop and implement a policy for the effective education of the most able science students, with the support of the head of department.

- Provide support for the identification of able pupils.

- Match the schemes of work to the needs of the able pupils.

- Provide guidance on teaching and learning methods to meet the needs of the most able.

- Share challenging targets for pupils and staff.

- Collect and collate data on able students.

- Monitor achievement and underachievement, and have systems in place to act on both.

- Evaluate provision and attainment and use this information to help with subsequent planning for improvement.

- Encourage continuing professional development for all staff.

- Develop effective links with other schools, the local community, business and industry in order to extend the science curriculum, enhance teaching and learning and develop pupils' wider understanding.

The subject teachers' roles and responsibilities in relation to the most able students

Subject teachers will be responsible for:

- the identification of able students

- monitoring the performance of individual able students within their teaching groups

- the provision of challenging and purposeful differentiated tasks

- setting appropriate homework tasks (e.g. pupils to pursue their own research/alternative methods of presentation)

- providing quality teaching and learning to meet the needs of the most able.

- developing students' wider understanding of science in our world.

From *Meeting the Needs of Your Most Able Pupils: Science*, Routledge 2008

> # Auditing provision for the most able students in science at KS3/4

Many schools will have used the subject audit that accompanies the Key Stage 3 National Strategy. This audit uses some of the strategies included in that document but also includes others that relate directly to provision for the most able.

Stage 1

Composition of the more able cohort in your department/subject

Once you have identified your top 5–10% (your more able or gifted and talented cohort) in each year group, look critically at the composition of that cohort to see whether any groups of pupils are under-represented in your subject.

	Y7	Y8	Y9	Y10	Y11
% of pupils in each year group who receive free school meals					
% of pupils in the more able cohort who receive free school meals					
% of boys in each year group					
% of boys in the more able cohort in each year group					
% of girls in each year group					
% of girls in the more able cohort in each year group					
% of ethnic minority pupils in each year group					
% of ethnic minority pupils in the more able cohort in each year group					

Current levels of attainment

Science

Year	Year 7 entry	End of KS3			End of KS4		
	% Level 5	% Level 6	% Level 7	% Level 8	% Bs	% As	% A*s
e.g. 2003							
e.g. 2004							
e.g. 2005							

Comparative levels of attainment

Science

Attainment in KS3 tests	Comparison with national averages		
	Above	In line	Below
% of pupils achieving Level 5 and above			
% of boys achieving Level 5 and above			
% of girls achieving Level 5 or above			
% of pupils achieving Level 6 and above			
% of boys achieving Level 6 or above			
% of girls achieving Level 6 or above			
% of pupils achieving Level 7 and above			
% of boys achieving Level 7 or above			
% of girls achieving Level 7 or above			
VA score for Science KS2–3			
VA score for Science KS3–4			
VA score for Science KS2–4			

Take-up of subjects at GCSE and post-16

Science

Subject	% of pupils going on to study this subject at A or AS level	% of boys going on to study this subject at A or AS level	% of girls going on to study this subject at A or AS level

Non-core subjects

Subject	% of pupils taking subject at KS4	% of boys taking subject at KS4	% of girls taking subject at KS4

Subject	% of pupils taking subject post-16	% of boys taking subject post-16	% of girls taking subject post-16

In general, how do the most able pupils react to the subject?

(a) Enthusiastic	(b) Non-committal	(c) Disengaged

If (b) or (c), can you pinpoint why?

....

....

....

Extracurricular

What extracurricular support/activities are provided for the most able in each year group? (Include clubs, masterclasses, extension classes, visits, invited experts, links with business/colleges, etc.)

Year	Extracurricular support/activity
Year 7	
Year 8	
Year 9	
Year 10	
Year 11	

General

Points to consider	Yes/No/In progress	Priority for Action
1. Has the department developed a policy on its provision for the more able?		
2. Does it have a more able/G&T coordinator or representative who liaises directly with the school more able/G&T coordinator?		
3. Are the most able students clearly identified in subject registers?		
4. Has the department identified CPD requirements in relation to more able pupils?		
5. Has the department agreed the strategies it will use to provide suitable pace, depth and breadth for the most able?		
6. Does the department have an agreed approach to providing for the exceptional child whose needs might not easily be met in the ordinary classroom?		
7. Does short-term planning outline expectations for the most able and any extended/modified tasks for them?		
8. Are there suitable resources for the most able?		
9. Is homework used to extend the most able?		
10. Do the most able have plenty of opportunities to develop as independent learners?		
11. Are different learning styles taken into account when planning for and assessing the most able?		
12. Do you keep a portfolio of outstanding work in your department?		
13. Is provision for the most able regularly discussed at departmental meetings?		
14 Do you share good practice in more able provision with other departments or schools?		
15. Is the progress of your most able students effectively monitored?		

Stage 2

Highlight all areas where achievement or provision in your department is lacking. Decide on about three priorities to raise standards or improve provision for your most able and draw up an action plan making it clear:

- what your success criteria are or what you hope to achieve

- what action will be taken

- when the action will be taken and by whom

- where you will go for help

- what resources you need

- how you will monitor your progress

- what your deadline is for assessing your success.

From *Meeting the Needs of Your Most Able Pupils: Science*, Routledge 2008

Departmental action plan for improving provision for the most able

Priority	Success criteria	Actions	When?	By whom?	Resources/support agencies
1.					
					Review Date
2.					
					Review Date
3.					
					Review Date

From *Meeting the Needs of Your Most Able Pupils: Science*, Routledge 2008

Appendix 2.3

Science individual learning plan

Name:		Form:
SATs sub-level achieved:	SATs target (2+levels):	GCSE target:
Areas of strength identified by staff:		
Areas of strength identified by pupil:		
Preferred method of learning:		
Pastoral support requirements:		
Curricular targets: 1. 2. 3.		
Extracurricular targets:		

From *Meeting the Needs of Your Most Able Pupils: Science*, Routledge 2008

Coursework writing frame

Planning

Aim – The aim of my experiment is . . .

Equipment – To do my experiment I will need . . .

Plan – I will do the experiment like this . . .

Safety – I will make my experiment safe by . . .

Fair test – I will only change this one thing . . .
      I will keep these the same . . .

Range – The range of readings I will take will be between . . .

      I will take . . . readings.

      I will do each reading . . . times.

Prediction – The thing I am going to change in my experiment is the . . .

When I change this I will see that . . .

I think this will happen because . . .

Observing

Recording – In my results table I will show . . .

Units – The units for my results will be . . .

Results table – My results table is drawn below . . .

Accurate recording – Now that I have done my experiment I think I can show my results more clearly below . . .

Analysis

Graph drawing – My graph is shown on the graph paper.

Findings – My results show that . . .

Graph reading – You can see from my graph that . . .

Evidence – The results show that my prediction was . . .

  The evidence for this is shown by . . .

  The scientific explanation for this is . . .

Evaluation

Reflecting – My experiment worked well because . . .

Odd results – An odd result I noticed was . . .

I expected this result to be . . .

I think this result could be explained by . . .

Improvements – I would describe my experiment as being . . .

I think I could improve the experiment by . . .

Reliability – I know my results were reliable because . . .

Therefore I can say my conclusion is . . .

The support and evidence for my conclusion comes from . . .

From *Meeting the Needs of Your Most Able Pupils: Science*, Routledge 2008

Preferred learning styles – a quick questionnaire

Answer each question by putting a V, A or K in the final column: V = visual, A = auditory, K = kinaesthetic.

When you spell do you . . .	V see the word? A sound the word? K write the word down to check it feels right?	
When you remember specific incidents do you . . .	V see well-focused colour pictures? A hear sounds first? K see a few pictures with movement in them?	
When you are thinking really hard and concentrating, are you distracted by . . .	V untidiness? A noise? K movement?	
When you are angry do you . . .	V silently seethe inside? A shout and scream? K clench fists, grit teeth and go away angry?	
When you forget someone or something do you . . .	V forget the name, not the face? A forget the face, not the name? K remember them by where, when and what you did?	
When you are reading do you . . .	V enjoy reading description and make your own picture? A hear the characters talking? K like to act it out?	
When you are relaxing do you . . .	V watch TV, read or see a play? A listen to music? K play sports or games?	
When you are learning do you prefer . . .	V work written and drawn in many colours? A to listen to instructions or a lecture? K to participate, make or do?	
When you are talking do you . . .	V talk little and don't like to listen for long? A like to listen and talk? K talk with hands and use gestures?	
When receiving praise do you prefer to . . .	V receive a written note? A hear it said to you? K be given a hug or pat on the back?	
Add up your scores	V = A = K =	

Which is your preferred learning style?

 From *Meeting the Needs of Your Most Able Pupils: Science*, Routledge 2008

Teaching styles and techniques

This questionnaire has been designed to encourage staff to consider their own teaching styles and techniques. In addition to this is the need to plan for inspection and collate evidence. With this in mind, it is worth retaining the responses to these questions and evidence from students' work. This will also support requests for training.

What is my predominant teaching style?

1. I deliver information to pupils.

2. The pupils work on their own with information I have given them.

3. The pupils work on their own with specific tasks for each.

4. The pupils work in groups with each group given a differentiated task.

5. The pupils work in pairs on whole-class questions.

6. The class discusses or does practical work with me.

Which of the above do I consider to be most effective in supporting students' learning? Can I say why?

Which of the above do I consider to be the least effective in supporting students' learning? Can I say why?

Am I regularly challenging the most able students in my teaching groups?

Can I show evidence of the ways that I challenge the most able?

Which of the following do I use within my lessons?

1. Differentiated work to match all abilities.

2. Guidance rather than telling students.

3. Guide students to independent learning.

4. Provide opportunities for research.

5. Encourage students to make and test predictions.

6. Challenge students to analyse the topic they are learning.

7. Challenge students to apply learning in new circumstances.

8. Encourage students to be critical of their own work.

9. Encourage students to evaluate their own learning styles.

> What is the most effective way for me to differentiate within the classroom?

Is the homework I give differentiated for the learner?

> If yes, can I give some examples of differentiated homework that I have given? If no, could I suggest some ideas, tasks or opportunities to do so?

Am I aware of the preferred learning styles of the learners in my class?
Do I provide opportunities in my lessons for:

- visual learners

- auditory learners

- kinaesthetic learners

so that each can access the learning in the lesson effectively?

> Can I show that I support all learning styles within my classroom? What examples could I give?

Remember to collate evidence. Photocopy work from students' books, worksheets that have been used, schemes of work that have been adapted. Keep all the responses to these questions and review them regularly to help improve provision for your most able learners.

 From *Meeting the Needs of Your Most Able Pupils: Science*, Routledge 2008

Lesson plan pro-forma

UNIT: LESSON:

Learning objectives (including skills)

-

-

Key words

Starter

Main

Plenary

All must

Most should

Some could

Apparatus/resources

Assessment (should refer to learning objectives)

Risks

Homework

From *Meeting the Needs of Your Most Able Pupils: Science*, Routledge 2008

References

Achter, J. A., Benbow, C. P. and Lubinski, D. (1997) 'Rethinking multipotentiality among the intellectually gifted: A critical review and recommendations'. *Gifted Pupil Quarterly*, **41**, 5–15.

Bloom, B. (ed.) (1956) *Taxonomy of Educational Objectives*. New York, Longmans, Green & Co.

Bloom, B. (ed.) (1985) *Developing Talent in Young People*. New York: Basic Books.

Campbell, L. (1997) Variations on a theme – how teachers interpret MI theory. *Educational Leadership*, 55 (1), 14–19.

Coates, D. and Eyre, D. (1999) 'Can encouraging the use of higher order thinking skills in science help young able children achieve more highly?'. Fourth Summer Conference for Teacher Education in Primary Science, Durham University.

Coates, D. and Wilson, H. (2000) 'Science masterclasses for able children in Year 2'. SCICentre 2000 and ASET Conference report, compiled by McKeon, F., SCICentre, University of Leicester.

Department for Education and Skills (1997) *Excellence in Schools*. London: DfES.

Department for Education and Employment (1998) *Health and Safety of Pupils on Educational Visits: A Good Practice Guide*. London: DfEE.

Department for Education and Skills (2001) *Health and Safety: Responsibilities and Powers*. 0803/2001. London: DfES.

Department for Education and Skills (2002) *Standards for LEAs in Overseeing Educational Visits. Supplement to Health and Safety of Pupils on Educational Visits: A Good Practice Guide*. 0564/2002. London: DfES.

Department for Education and Skills (2002) *Standards for Adventure. Supplement to Health and Safety of Pupils on Educational Visits: A Good Practice Guide*. 0565/2002. London: DfES.

Department for Education and Skills (2002) *KS3 National Strategy – Learning Styles and Writing in Science*. DfES 0384/2002. London: DfES (available at www.standards.dfes.gov.uk/keystage3/downloads/ks3learnstyle_sco38402.pdf).

Eyre, D. (1997) *Able Children in Ordinary Schools*. London: David Fulton Publishers.

Gardner, H. (1993) *Frames of Mind: the Theory of Multiple Intelligences*, 10th annual edn. New York: Basic Books.

Gardner, H. (1999) *Intelligence Reframed: Multiple intelligences for the 21st Century*. New York: Basic Books.

Gardner, H. (2000) 'The giftedness matrix: a developmental perspective' in Friedman, R. C. and Shore, B. M. (eds), *Talents Unfolding: Cognition and Development*. Washington DC: American Psychological Association.

Langrehr, J. (2001) *Teaching Our Children to Think*. Indiana, USA: National Educational Service.

Ofsted (2003) *Handbook for Inspecting Secondary Schools.* London: Ofsted. (An HTML version is available at www.ofsted.gov.uk/publications/docs/hb2003/sechb03/hmi1360-01.html)

Ofsted (2003) *Inspection of Local Education Authorities; Ofsted/Audit Commission Inspection Guidance.* December 2003 v1a.

Renzulli, J. S. (1978) What Makes Giftedness? Re-examining a Definition. *Phi Delta Kappan,* **60** (3), 180–184, 186.

Further information

Department for Education and Skills (DfES)

Chief Medical Officer's advice on farm visits, Department of Health Press Notice, 12 April 2000.

Child Protection: Preventing Unsuitable People from Working with Children and Young Persons in the Education Service, 2002

Guidance on First Aid for Schools (www.teachernet.gov.uk/firstaid)

Health and Safety of Pupils on Educational Visits: A Good Practice Guide (HASPEV) and its three supplements (www.teachernet.gov.uk/visits)

Health and Safety: Responsibilities and Powers (www.teachernet.gov.uk/responsibilities)

Safety Education Guidance Leaflet (www.teachernet.gov.uk/safetyeducation guidance)

Supporting Pupils with Medical Needs: A Good Practice Guide (www.teachernet.gov.uk/medical)

Work Experience: a Guide for Employers, 2002

Work Experience: a Guide for Secondary Schools, 2002

Health and Safety Executive (HSE)

A Guide to Risk Assessment Requirements (www.hse.gov.uk/pubns/indg218.pdf)

Adventure Activities Centres – Five Steps to Risk Assessment

Avoiding Ill Health at Open Farms: Advice to Teachers, AIS23 (new edition on 28 June 2000 of advice mentioned in HASPEV)

Five Steps to Risk Assessment (www.hse.gov.uk/pubns/indg163.pdf)

Guidance to the Licensing Authority on the Adventure Activities Licensing Regulations 1996

Managing Health and Safety in Swimming Pools, revised edition 1999, HSG 179

Preparing Young People for a Safer Life (issued with Cheshire County Council and The Institute of Occupational Safety and Health – tel. 0116 257 3100). This has a model risk assessment for a sponsored walk.

Reducing Risk Protecting People, 2001

Statement of Risk Perception in Adventure and Outdoor Activities, Adventure Activities Industry Advisory Committee (AAIAC)

The New General Teaching Requirement for Health and Safety, 1999

Others

Educational Visits, NASUWT, 2001

Get Safe for Summer, Amateur Swimming Association (www.asa-awards.co.uk)

Guidance is produced by many of the voluntary youth organisations.

Guidance published by the National Governing Bodies (NGBs) for various adventure activities as in HASPEV. NGBs also maintain leader training and assessment programmes.

Guidelines for Off-Site Educational Visits and Activities in the United Kingdom, Nottinghamshire CC, September 2001, has a section on camping.

Information about adventure activity providers covered by the Adventure Activities Licensing Scheme (www.aala.org.uk)

Minibus Safety: A Code of Practice, RoSPA and others, 2002 (www.rospa.com/roadsafety/info/minibus_code.pdf)

Safe and Responsible Expeditions and Guidelines for Youth Expeditions, Young Explorers' Trust (www.rgs.org/eacpubs)

Safe Kids Campaign Report 2000, Child Accident Prevention Trust

Safe Supervision for Teaching and Coaching Swimming, Amateur Swimming Association and others, 2nd edition, 2001, tel. 01509 618700. Advice on ratios in HASPEV paragraph 187, which are pupil year-based, should be read in conjunction with the competence-based ratios in this document.

Safety on School Trips – A Teachers and the Law Booklet, The Professional Association of Teachers, revised edition, 2002

The British Activity Holiday Association, 22 Green Lane, Hersham, Surrey, KT12 5HD, tel./fax 01932 252994 (www.baha.org.uk)

The Duke of Edinburgh's Award has its own clear structure, procedures and guidelines (www.theaward.org)

The Independent Schools Adventure Activities Association (ISAAA) offers help, support and technical advice to any Independent School (isaaa.org.uk)

The OCR (Oxford Cambridge and RSA Examinations) 'Off-Site Safety Management Scheme' provides a training course aimed at those who organise off-site visits. It is exam-based and teachers can combine it with practical experience. (www.ocr.org.uk)

The Royal Geographical Society (with IBG)'s Expedition Advisory Centre, 1 Kensington Gore, London SW7 2AR, provides advice, information and training to anyone planning an overseas expedition, tel. 020 7591 3030 (www.rgs.org/eac)

The Royal Life Saving Society UK, River House, High St, Broom, Warwickshire, B50 4HN, tel. 01789 773994 (www.lifesavers.org.uk)

The Suzy Lamplugh Trust has produced a range of guidance on personal safety, including booklets, videos and training courses (www.suzylamplugh.org)

The Wales Tourist Board, the Scottish Tourist Board and the British Activity Holiday Association provide voluntary inspection schemes to complement licensing for providers of activities that are outside the scope of licensing.

The Waterways Code (leaflet) and *The Waterways Code for Boaters* (video) are available from British Waterways, tel. 01923 01120 (www.british waterways.co.uk)

Transport for London provides free transport for school groups on the underground, buses, Thameslink and the Docklands Light Railway. The advice line for the scheme is 020 7918 3954 and the website is at www.tfl.gov.uk/

schoolparty. The general travel advice line can offer information on route planning and station layouts. Apart from its commitment to the safety of its passengers Transport for London does not offer specific advice on health and safety for school groups but refers them to HASPEV and HSE risk assessment guidance.